P9-APU-472

RADICAL HOSPITALITY

Benedict's Way of Love

*Father Daniel Homan, O.S.B.,
and Lonni Collins Pratt*

PARACLETE PRESS
BREWSTER, MASSACHUSETTS

2006 *Third Paperback Printing*
2005 *First and Second Paperback Printing*
2002 *First Hardcover Printing*

© 2002 by Lonni Collins Pratt and Daniel Homan, O.S.B.

ISBN 10: 1-55725-441-9
ISBN 13: 978-1-55725-441-2

Library of Congress Cataloging–in–Publication Data
Pratt, Loni Collins, 1953–

Radical hospitality : Benedict's way of love / Loni Collins Pratt and
Daniel Homan.

p.   cm.
ISBN 1–55725–441–9

1. Hospitality—Religious aspects—Christianity. 2. Benedict, Saint,
Abbot of Monte Cassino. Regula. I. Homan, Daniel, O.S.B. II. Title.
BV4647.H67 P73   2002
241'.671—dc21   2002009673

Excerpts from the Rule of St. Benedict are taken from *The Rule of St.
Benedict in Latin and English with Notes*, The Liturgical Press,
Collegeville, MN, 1981.

10 9 8 7 6 5 4 3

All rights reserved. No portion of this book may be reproduced, stored in
an electronic retrieval system, or transmitted in any form or by any
means—electronic, mechanical, photocopy, recording, or any other—
except for brief quotations in printed reviews, without the prior permission
of the publisher.

Published by Paraclete Press
Brewster, Massachusetts
www.paracletepress.com

Printed in the United States of America.

To Br. Benedict Giuliani, O.S.B.,
an inspiration to us both.

To my mother, Mary Elizabeth Brennan Homan,
Irish to the core. My father was German
and she loved him, but she always told us
that our hearts were Irish. Who knows?
Between them they taught us,
long before I ever heard of St. Benedict,
to see the Christ in everyone.

To my husband, David,
who never forgets how to love.

"All guests who present themselves are to be welcomed as Christ, for he himself will say: 'I was a stranger and you welcomed me.'"

  —The Rule of St. Benedict 53:1

"Once a guest has been announced, the superior and the community are to meet the guest with all the courtesy of love."

  —The Rule of St. Benedict 53:3

"Great care and concern are to be shown in receiving poor people and pilgrims, because in them more particularly Christ is received. . . ."

  —The Rule of St. Benedict 53:15

"Let us open our eyes to the deifying light, let us hear with attentive ears the warning which the divine voice cries daily to us, 'Today if you hear his voice, harden not your hearts.'"

  —The Rule of St. Benedict, Prologue 29

contents

introduction

Introduction

Maybe you are happiest when sharing your table, or your space, with a guest. Maybe you yearn for connections to others. Maybe you are startled by the deep well of cynicism you've discovered in yourself and you want to stop keeping people at a distance. Maybe you, like many others, are looking for ways to heal from the horror of terrorism. Maybe you're curious about monasticism and the spirituality of monasticism.

Monasticism has much to teach us about welcoming and connecting with others. In exploring the deeper meaning of hospitality in these pages, we will be using the Benedictine path of hospitality as a model. Hospitality is at the center of what it means to be a monk.

You have your own reasons for being interested in the subject of welcoming others, and it may or may not have anything to do with spirituality. It is impossible to discuss true hospitality without delving into spirituality. Spirituality is essential to this discussion because spirituality is essential to what it means to be human. The human spirit is home to our deepest desires and darkest fears. It is also the place from which you yearn for a hand that will reach for yours. We both want and fear connecting with each other. Our resistance to others, resistance to change—these are housed in the mysterious realm of spirit. Our minds cannot conceive of solutions to our dilemma until our hearts are convinced to love. Because our ambivalence over connections with others is a problem of the heart and the spirit, the discussion will be largely spiritual.

When St. Benedict wrote of hospitality he stressed the importance of welcoming the outsider, the poor, the pilgrim. Benedict understood that guests are crucial to the making of a monk. Benedict was a realist; he knew there would always be people at the monastery door. This was not a dreary reality for which he had to make allowances; it was a means of grace given to his monks, and he taught them how this complicated reality contributed to the making of a heart.

Guests are crucial to the making of any heart. Benedict instructed his monks to welcome the Divine in the stranger. He told them to look again, look deeper when you look into the eyes of stranger. If you want to be a person of great spirit, you can't do life alone. If spirituality matters to you, you can't do spirituality alone either. To really grow as a human being you need other people. This conviction permeates Benedict's Rule.

The monasteries of Benedict's time fifteen centuries ago were small. Usually they housed about a dozen monks, making the monastery something like a large family. They gathered as a Christian household to live and grow toward the Divine together. To guide them in this effort, Benedict crafted a simple, short document called *The Rule of St. Benedict*. It is no more than nine thousand words long, divided into seventy-three short pages. An average person can read it in about an hour. The *Rule* has endured for the past fifteen hundred years and shapes most of Western monasticism. For this reason, St. Benedict is considered by most to be the father of Western monasticism.

Hospitality is at the center of what it means to be a monk. But, Benedict didn't come up with the idea. The *Rule* is based on the teachings of Jesus. Jesus. Not a new improved guru for the new millennium, but the same old Jesus that the Church has tried to follow for two thousand years.

A little boy was leaving a Christmas service with his father and paused at the manger outside the church. He looked at it, tilted his head for another angle, and then said to his father, "It's the same Jesus we had last year. Can't we get a new Jesus?" The father smiled and squatted next to his son. He was silent a couple of seconds and then said, "Son, we're Christians. We get the same Jesus every Christmas. That's how it works."

In monasticism you don't get a trendy new Jesus, you get the same old Jesus everyone gets. That's how it works. The monks who have become spiritual and social guides for so many are not practicing a new religion; they practice a very old one, the religion based on the life of Jesus. Benedict wrote the *Rule* within the context of his Christian faith, and so his teachings cannot be separated from the teachings of Jesus.

The word *rule* is something of a problem for us. We automatically resist rules. It is a symptom of contemporary life. Try thinking about it this way: A rule is nothing more than a set of ideas to help you determine the kind of person you will be and the course of your

life. These ideas will be the reason you form certain habits (exercising, paying your bills on time, eating toast in the morning, meditating, and so on).

We all have some sort of rule we live by, consciously or otherwise. Your own rule consists of the little things you do that shape your life. The desire for balance or inner calm, the yearning for a life that feels right: These are the reasons we live by some kind of collected wisdom. Your rule of life is nothing more than what you have determined is most important to seeking and maintaining a meaningful existence. Your rule is a collection of what you think matters: I must be faithful to my friends, I must exercise, I must save money, I must take a couple of hours each week to be alone, I must make time to be with the people I love.

Your rule is what makes your life worthwhile. It is an expression of how you are spending your energy. It indicates what you value most. Your rule is the glue that holds your life together. By your rule you make choices about how you will spend your time and resources, you make choices about how you will spend yourself.

In a monastery, where people come together as strangers from a wide variety of backgrounds, some sort of unifying system is necessary. That is the purpose of Benedict's *Rule*.

The Rule in a monastery holds the place together. It is a central, organizing wisdom for monks who are trying to build a life together pointing toward God. The Rule provides guidance, and it interprets gospel values in a way that is distinctive to Benedictines. In a family, we would probably consider the values shared by a man and woman a similar commonality upon which a life can be built.

The Rule of St. Benedict is not a set of rules or laws. We miss the essence of this ancient writing when we approach it in some literalistic sense. Rather, it is a collection of wisdom that has endured the hard blows of constant change in the last fifteen hundred years. There is no shortage of monastic rules, but only Benedict's *Rule* has thrived. It is uncomplicated wisdom that can build a life and expand a heart.

Many ways of life nurture the practice of hospitality. Monasticism isn't the only model. Many people who have never heard of Benedict practice a deep hospitality. Nor do we claim that any of the strengths we describe are unique to monasticism. Instead, we assert that monasticism is a healthy way of creating a life that values what is most important. Respect for human beings is not merely honored by the Benedictine tradition; it comes to life within the person who attempts to enter the tradition. In these pages we hope to open a door to a hospitable way of life.

The Rule of St. Benedict begins with an invitation to listen. "Listen carefully, my child, to the instructions of the spiritual master, and attend to them with the ear of your heart. This is advice from a father who loves you; welcome it, and faithfully put it into practice."

This is the core of monastic life. *Listen.* At the beginning, you are invited to open your ears, open your heart, and listen for wisdom, listen for a Voice, listen for the *more* that is woven into all that is. That is what we invite you to do: listen.

Benedictine spirituality has a distinct ethos, which is learned through contact with the monks, through engaging with their way of life. Not everyone has a monastery down the road, however, so in these pages we would like to introduce you to St. Benedict Monastery, where one of us, Father Dan, lives. We will introduce you to some of the monks there and hope that you will like them. We invite you to make the monastery your home for a little while.

St. Benedict Monastery is located in Oxford, Michigan, several miles up a gravel road that weaves toward the top of a hill at about twelve hundred feet above sea level. The setting was a glorious one long before religious orders made homes in this part of Michigan. Native Americans spoke of it as being sacred. Sensitive people are often aware of this sense of holiness present in the setting.

Father Noel has been with God for several years now. But when we talk about Benedictine hospitality, he is an example that we both remember, for different reasons.

Father Noel and Father Dan were taking a walk on the monastery grounds one day. It was the kind of day made for a walk with a friend. A group of eleven- and twelve-year-olds from an institution for troubled children were on a tour of the monastery. They had arrived by hay wagon, pulled by horses with a couple of young drivers, probably in their late teens.

Acres of rolling grass invite you to stretch out on a sultry summer day and enjoy the soft grass and warm earth. The monastery grounds are well groomed, but the place doesn't feel like an institution.

It is home to the Benedictines, and a home is what it feels like—an easy place to be. Something about the place is welcoming.

The two monks were enjoying one of those long, warm days of late summer. Guests were not as common in those days, but when they showed up they were welcome. Occupied in conversation, Father Dan did not notice the hay wagon drivers until they came within a few yards.

"I was stopped in my tracks," he remembers. "Right there on the yard in front of us, the two wagon drivers were passing a joint back and forth, looking completely at home, as if this was the most natural thing to do at a monastery. In case you're wondering, it isn't."

Father Noel, born in Italy and a monk all of his adult life, had never seen marijuana. He was not a naïve or stupid man; such a thing simply was not part of his experience. Father Dan was a street-smart kid raised in Detroit. Before he could demand an explanation, Father Noel spoke up.

"Young men," he exclaimed with wide-armed relish, "we are so glad that you are with us today to enjoy the grass."

It was an enthusiastic and heartfelt welcome from the hospitable soul of an old monk. The guys naturally thought he was one very cool old monk.

It would never have occurred to Father Noel to be suspicious of the young men. While many people would have considered them intruders, his welcome could not have been more sincere. He was delighted to see the children of God enjoying the expansive grounds. He was very happy to see someone enjoying the grass of the monastery.

Lonni met Father Noel when she was a guest at a friend's simple profession as a monk. A simple profession is the first set of vows a monk takes early in his monastic life. Following the solemn ceremony, a party that includes family and close friends is common. On this occasion, good friends of the monastic community had prepared a wonderful meal. During dinner, Lonni was seated between the newly professed monk and Father Dan. Dan was seated between Lonni and Noel. The conversation was jovial and constant.

Father Noel's Italian accent remained thick until the day he died, so, the hospitable thing to do, thought Father Dan, was to make sure that Lonni understood him. Since he was sitting between them, Dan considered himself in the perfect spot to do so.

Throughout the meal, he translated Noel's conversation in a whisper to Lonni while the older monk talked with a lively animation, smiling most of the time. Father Noel had not met the guest before, and being Benedictine, he was eager to extend a welcome and get to know her a bit. Hospitality is at the core of Benedictine spirituality, and Noel was Benedictine to the marrow.

After the dinner, Dan wandered off to greet guests. He did not notice as Father Noel found Lonni while she talked with a small group of women. He did not notice Noel waiting for his moment to speak to her, without Dan's assistance.

Lonni told Dan later that Father Noel had taken her hands and said to her with a wide grin, "Now we can really talk, eh. . . . ," as he motioned toward Dan, the obstacle seated between them. He not only wanted to be hospitable, he wanted to do so without a middleman.

Father Noel's response to the guest at the table and the guest on the lawn flowed from him naturally; it had been fostered by a lifetime of making himself open to the stranger. To him, hospitality was not about social graces but about mutual reverence. Father Noel knew that spirituality is about relationships. Every man, woman, and child bears to us the presence of God.

Manners and civility, however, are not at the heart of Benedictine hospitality, although we of course hope monks will not be rude or inconsiderate. Forget about turned-down sheets, mints on the pillow, and towel-warmers. Monastic hospitality creates sacred space where the guest is free to be alone, to enter silence, to pray and rest. No one is compelled to fill up the guest's spare time or set an agenda for him or her. Hospitality is openhanded. It's definitely not summer camp, but more like a refugee center for the traveler who needs shelter from the thieves along the way.

If you are visiting a monastery and need someone to talk to, you will usually find an available ear, but they won't line up at your door to volunteer. The monks aren't there to keep anyone occupied or to be entertaining. Instead, Benedict tells us to offer an open heart, a stance of availability, and to look for God lurking in every single person who comes through the door. Monks do not consider themselves somehow polluted by contact with others. They aren't in a monastery to avoid people. This is a common misunderstanding of monastic life.

Monastic hospitality is devoted to the vision of unity among God's children. It is a necessary developmental vision for the monk because he will achieve no higher relationship with God, or others, than the one he achieves with himself. A monk's life presents us with a paradox. His life is a witness to us that, ultimately, we are all alone. We live and die alone. We wake up with only ourselves. We are never as fully understood and are never loved as well as we long to be.

On the other hand, the monk, to be a monk, needs people. He grows through encounters with others. He learns about himself as he is loved, annoyed, grieved, respected—all in community and with the guest. To think of the monk as only a solitary is a mistaken notion. There is a great truth to the monk as a solitary, as one who lives alone with God, but that aloneness is not lived apart. It is lived in community.

Recently Lonni was leading a retreat for a group of United Methodist women and their guests. It was an overnight event. Most retreatants find the silence of a retreat difficult the first day. She noticed this was not true for this group; they sank into the silence as if it were a big, overstuffed chair where they were joyfully content to remain.

After dinner she was in the retreat house library. It was a free time, and on most such retreats the women would use the period to socialize. She was surprised when a group of fifteen or so women found her in the library, joined her, and shot so many questions at her about monastic life that she could not keep up with them. Something about the monastic way of life speaks to us. We sense, on a soul level, that monasteries tell us something important about how to live in times like these.

Monasticism was becoming popular, and you might even say monks were becoming trendy prior to September 11, 2001. Looking back, it is sometimes difficult to remember what the world was like prior to that event. There were lots of trends: "reality" television, for example. The television show *Who Wants to be a Millionaire* was so popular it was on several nights each week. Such trends came and went, revealing how profoundly bored and empty Americans felt. And then it all changed. Within an hour of the collapse of the second tower of the World Trade Center, a woman on the streets of New York looked into a camera and said, "Nothing is ever going to be the same again."

Dan was in Rome watching those unforgettable events unfold and remembers thinking, "She's right, she's absolutely right, but I wish she were wrong."

What was trendy hardly seemed to matter anymore. Suddenly people were not as interested in "virtual reality" because reality had become more than enough.

On September 10, it was considered spiritually enlightened to say, "I'm a spiritual person but I'm not into organized religion." But when Americans needed an anchor, something to hold onto, they headed for the staying power of tradition. They filled churches, mosques, and synagogues in record numbers. Monasticism is undeniably part of organized religion. It has stood the test of time. America is looking to what has endured, at a time when it seems the very foundations of the world have been rocked.

Benedict lived in the same kind of chaos. He wrote to a culture shaken to the core by the fall of the Roman Empire, fifteen hundred years ago. This makes Benedict particularly timely. People are now mining Benedictine spirituality to its depths for the profound wisdom that has made it relevant all these centuries.

The stranger next door, and at our door, is particularly frightening. We won't dodge the difficult reality of actual danger. People have been hurt by strangers. You need only to turn on the evening news to be aware that we are growing into a fearful people, suspicious of strangers and outsiders. When we speak of the depth of hospitality, we are proposing something scary and radical. But it's worth the risk. Unless we find a way to open ourselves to others, we will grow even more isolated and frightened. If we do not find and practice ways of hospitality we will grow increasingly hostile. Hospitality is the answer to hostility. Jesus said to love your neighbor; hospitality is how.

The people we encounter daily, at the gas station and grocery store and flower shop, aren't incidental to our lives. Benedict teaches us that if we close ourselves to the stranger, we close ourselves to the Sacred. If we lock our doors and bolt our gates, we are forbidding God to come to us. And never before have we needed so badly to know that God comes to us.

Most of us have heard some version of the Good Samaritan story from the Gospels of the New Testament. Jesus told a story. A traveler is accosted, robbed, beaten, and left to die. The dying man is ignored, as he suffers on the side of the road, by the "right" kind of people, acceptable people with solid values and important priorities.

These are people like us. They have things to do. They are trying very hard to get it all done. They aren't vicious people, but they do consider caution a virtue.

It was the "wrong" kind of person, in the culture of the New Testament—a Samaritan—who stopped to help. The Samaritan went the extra mile and put himself on the line. He gave his time, energy, and resources. When we say "The Good Samaritan," we are saying, "The Good but Completely Unacceptable Foreigner."

The story is about us, and it is about strangers. We are called to be the kind stranger, to be kind to strangers, and to hold our breaths in wonder at the healing power of the stranger among us. The story is also a reminder that every one of us is going to be the one beaten up and waiting for healing at the side of the road. You don't have to live long before you realize that no one escapes pain.

We moderns have been ambushed by technology along the way, and we've been beaten up by the media. We, who are consumers, have discovered that in our constant consuming we are leaving little for anyone else and we're losing our souls. We find ourselves scattered on the winds of change to places we never wanted to go. Our lives seem to be spinning out of control. It is no wonder we lock our doors and switch on the security system.

Go with us to a corner of the sprawling market in Mexico City where an old Indian man named Pota-lamo is selling onions. Twenty strings of onions lay in front of him. A guy from Denver walks up and asks, "How much for a string of onions?"

"Ten cents," replies Pota-lamo.

"How much for two strings?"

Pota-lamo fixes his eyes on him and says, "Twenty cents."

"What about three?"

"Thirty cents."

"Not much of a reduction for quantity. Would you take twenty-five cents for three?"

"No."

"Well, how much for all of it, the whole twenty strings?"

"I will not sell you the whole twenty strings."

"Why not?" asks the American. "Aren't you here to sell onions?"

"No," replies Pota-lamo, "I am here to live my life. I love this market. I love the crowds. I love the sunlight and smells. I love the children. I love to have my friends come by and talk about their babies and their crops. That is my life and for that reason I sit here with my twenty strings of onions. If I sell all my onions to one customer, then my day is over and I have lost my life that I love—and that I will not do."

Living life in a way that places a higher value on relationships and community than it does on commerce and productivity—this is counter to how most of us have been taught. We live our lives selling onions. There is no room for hospitality in a life like that. We greet the morning sun each day with our to-do lists, while the monk greets the sun with prayer and silence.

We hide out, isolate ourselves, and deny our natural need for others. We erroneously think we need safety the most. What we need most is acceptance. You probably can't understand me, and I might not understand you, but we can accept each other. We need to connect and feel the deep acceptance of another human being and that will make the world feel safer. Locks and firewalls can never do for our tired souls what friendship and companionship do.

Acceptance. Now there's a word loaded with meaning. We tend to confuse it with tolerance or even approval. But acceptance is about receiving, rather than judging. The father, who will not visit his son because his son is living unmarried with a woman, or even another man, might say he doesn't want to condone his son's choices. We feel for him, but we know it's a cover-up because we, too, have rationalized our avoidance of things and situations we would rather not have to face. Then we can hide the disappointment, cover the anger, and justify the rejection. We struggle in our best efforts to hold back judgment and just accept. Acceptance is not about condoning; it is about embracing.

When we accept, we take an open stance to the other person. It is more than merely piously tolerating them. We stand in the same space and we appreciate who they are, right now at this moment, and affirm the Sacred in them. Monks do this better than most. Lonni has compared the acceptance given to her by the monks with a certain priest she knew a very long time ago.

She was six years old and days away from making her First Communion. At a rehearsal she and the other children practiced processing in and learning where to stand and how to take the host and return to their seats. Her brother Harry was one of the altar boys who would be assisting.

She remembers that the other children had gone home. Harry told her to stay put in the front row of the church and he'd be back in a few minutes. Sit still and stay put: not an easy thing for a six-year-old. Lonni remembers watching him disappear through the sacristy door and thinking that he might never emerge from that place of wonders and mystery.

She had not been seated long when Father Lawrence, the parish priest, found her there—alone. She explained that she was waiting for Harry so they could walk home together.

"Oh. Well, he's going to be a while. He's watering my plants." (That was code for having a cigarette with the other altar boys—things were different forty years ago.) Father Lawrence offered his hand, "Would you like to see the sacristy?"

How did he know, she wondered, that she wanted to see behind that closed door, that she wanted to go into the mystery? It was like the gates of heaven swinging open. Her face must have told him the answer. He pulled Lonni to her feet and they headed toward the altar before she could get words out. That crazy priest even let her hold a chalice. A little girl. A girl of all things.

Monks are a lot like old Father Lawrence. They accept others totally, no, not perfectly and not all the time—but they keep trying to take us into the hidden places and the holy mysteries we dream of knowing, but feel unprepared or unworthy to enter. It isn't that the monk has some special right to go into that place with us; it is just that a lifetime of facing himself makes a monk brave.

Monks break all our conventional rules in the way they love. It is their tradition. One of our favorite examples of this is how St. Benedict told his followers that if you have to discipline someone make sure you send a couple of wise monks to him to comfort him and be on his side (you do this on the sly) and "support the wavering brother." "Remember," Benedict tells his monks, ". . . you have undertaken care of the sick, not tyranny over the healthy." Benedict can seem tough and unrelenting, but he is unrelenting in love, acceptance, and reconciliation.

Hospitality tops the list of what is valued in a monastery because people are valued, and an equal dignity for all is assumed. Monks view people positively. Every human is sacred; every life is holy ground.

Many of the people who rattle the gates of St. Benedict Monastery arrive there in search of shelter. Lonni says this is true of her early experience with the monastery. She first went to visit a friend who was part of the monastic community. It was a difficult time for her. Her teenaged daughter had been in a near-fatal auto accident. During the same time Lonni became a target of gossip and rumor. She watched church people attacking each other. She watched church people destroying others. The world did not feel safe. Every trace of God was emptied from the universe. Each day she had to make herself get out of the bed, breathe in and out, and keep moving.

She writes of this time, "With the monks I was suddenly accepted—accepted during a time when I felt rejected, violated, misunderstood, and betrayed. I remained because these monks loved me without question. I didn't have to prove anything. I didn't have to be smart or witty, deep or cultured, beautiful or young. I just had to let them love me."

By accepting someone, we do what seems to be a small, ordinary thing. A single act would seem to be small anyway, but little acts of giving, one upon another, pile up to create a huge force capable of repelling darkness and transforming the world. A friendly conversation with a stranger at a bus stop can be the embodiment of hospitality. When we accept a human being, we are fostering the kind of hospitality that will change everything. When we build a life of acceptance, we build a new kind of kingdom among us.

A brief excerpt from Lonni's journal describes what the monastery has become for her:

> I've been at the monastery on bright winter mornings and lazy summer afternoons, sitting alone in the chapel that seems perched high at the edge of the world. If you gaze upward, past the soaring panels of glass behind the altar, you will see an overhang from the dramatic roofline. Birds swoop out from under the edge of the roof. They dive and rise and glide. Sometimes they even seem to hover and look at you through the endless glass with tree-covered hills as a backdrop.
>
> This high place is their home. They live sheltered and safe in a holy place where they have built their

nests and raise their young. The monastery is that for me—and for many others I've talked to—a sheltering holy place.

The monastic life has an essence that is worth observing, worth applying to your own complicated life. Yes, monastic lives are different, but not that different. Monks still have mouths to feed, windows to wash, groceries to buy, cars to repair, and complications to sort out. There are more similarities than differences.

The monk is not some otherworldly character; he's just a guy in a black robe who is trying very hard to be found by God. People are often tempted to make the monk into some spiritual Superman, but he will not be real to you unless he is human. What Christians call the Incarnation shows us that God knew no one becomes real to us unless they're human, including God.

Perhaps you have heard the song "Superman" by Five for Fighting. There are a few words in it that describe the monk pretty well: "I'm just a man in a funny red sheet, searching for something special inside of me." A monk will spend his life searching for what is special in all of us—the divine presence. He has bad days and good days the same as you do. Whatever is happening, the monk is called to stretch himself, without fail, to be open to the stranger and guest at the door.

A problem with using the monastic model as a guide for life is that it comes with language no one uses anymore. *Hospitality. Stability. Chastity. Poverty. Obedience.* Monks hold meetings they call diets, and they do not mean cutting calories. They have leaders who are called Primates and who don't live in the local zoo. What is a Prior? The leader of a monastic community; Father Dan is one. What does *the work of God* mean? How many ways can you use the word *cloister*?

We will try to be careful in using language that might be confusing. If you're familiar with things Benedictine this might seem unnecessary, but we ask you to remember the marvelous idea of hospitality as we attempt to make this book an open place for all of God's children.

Some might think of monasticism as too "traditional" to be of any meaning today. In a world where the word *tradition* is nearly obscene, monasticism shows us how humanizing and freeing tradition can be. Through tradition we receive the wisdom of those who have gone on before us. Tradition underscores that which we must not forget. Tradition is valuable, not because it is old and established but because it has endured and brought about much that is good.

Yet, there is always the possibility of the new and untried, of seeing the old in a new light. In fact, Benedict makes clear in the *Rule* that young people have something important to offer, and it is vital that we listen to the young with all their fresh ideas. The Benedictine way of life and hospitality is full of openness and risk.

Benedict's conviction was that all of us are headed together toward God. We are headed toward union with God. It is impossible to say what this means, exactly, but we live our little lives with big purpose and a sense that there is more. We do this by faith. It goes against the seeming ordinariness of everything. We take a radical position when we insist that it all *does* matter. Life is holy ground.

Now be careful about this. Holy ground is dangerous. It is the region of thundering mountains and burning bushes; it is the domain of men and women bellowing prophesy with fire in their wings and the winds of change in their voices. A friend from Alaska has said that lots of people visit the state in pursuit of great beauty and breathless awe. Expecting to be tackled by wonder and to experience some earth-shattering majesty, these people encounter long stretches of treacherous roads and miles of what looks like frozen desert. It teems with hidden dangers—like bears. After one couple was mauled, they told a reporter that they would never return to "this godforsaken" place. Holy places put you at risk more so than any other place. You feel both at risk and awed in a holy place.

In 1982, author Annie Dillard witnessed a total eclipse of the sun and described this awesome experience:

> The second before the sun went out, we saw a wall of dark shadow come speeding at us. We no sooner saw it than it was upon us, like thunder. It roared up the valley. It slammed our hill and knocked us out. It was the monstrous swift shadow cone of the moon. I have since read that this wave of shadow moves 1800 miles an hour. Language can give no sense of this sort of speed—1800 miles an hour. It was 195 miles wide. No end was in sight; you saw

only the edge. It rolled at you across land 1800 miles an hour, hauling darkness like plague behind it. Seeing it, and knowing it was coming straight for you, was like feeling a slug of anesthetic shoot up your arm. . . . We saw the wall of shadow coming, and screamed before it hit us.

Less than two minutes later, when the sun emerged, the trailing edge of the shadow cone sped away. . . . We blinked into the light. . . . When the sun appeared as a blinding bead on the ring's side, the eclipse was over . . . the real world began there. I remember now, we all hurried away. . . . We never looked back. It was a general vamoose . . . enough is enough. . . . From the depths of mystery, and even the heights of splendor, we bounce back and hurry for the latitudes of home. (from *The Annie Dillard Reader*)

Life is a lot like that hilltop. We gather together to have the hell scared out of us, literally. We catch a glimpse of each other, we sense the smell of God, and although we rush away from the holiest of moments, we are utterly changed. Life slams us into God, and if we have any sense knocked into us, we realize that behind all the ordinary stuff there is something more dazzling and real than we can understand. Life is holy ground. Holy ground is risky.

Benedict understands holy ground. Life is holy ground and so are the monastery, the monk, and the guest. The monastery is not personal property; it belongs to God.

Your life is not personal property; you belong to God. Benedict called the monastery God's house. The monks own nothing, they are simply stewards of whatever God gives them. In this vision, even the monks are guests, and so Benedict insists that the monks "serve one another in love." "Never give a hollow greeting of peace," he writes, "or turn away when someone needs your love."

At the monastery everyone is a guest, not just the visitor at the door, but the monks themselves. God is the host, but God also becomes the guest we receive in others. In the monastic image of the world, we are all guests, we are all travelers, we are all a little lost, and we are all looking for a place to rest a while.

A journey is one of the most common metaphors for life. We understand the image contains some strong truth. Life is very much like a journey. In our quiet moments, when we let down our guard, we become aware that we are looking for something, going somewhere, even though most of the time we cannot say where.

Even if you are born, grow up, and die in the same house in which your parents and grandparents spent their lives, life is still a journey. Saint Benedict wrote from his conviction that life truly is a journey and we are all cotravelers who need one another if we are to get home.

Every moment is more brightly precious than we can possibly understand. Our lives are worth more than the best deal that might tempt you to sell your soul. We did not bargain for most of what we get in this life, but life itself is worth holding onto, and worth valuing. It is a great loss if we greet every day with clenched hands stuffed with our own devices. We will never know what is out there waiting for us if we don't extend an empty hand to the world and wait for the wonder to happen. Benedictine hospitality provides us with a way to offer empty hands to the world. It provides us with a way home.

Sometimes we get so lost that we need a map. Without a point of reference we keep stumbling in circles with little awareness of where we've been, or how to reach where we are going. Monastic life provides one such point of reference. It provides us a way to find our way back to Love, when that possibility seems about as remote as the North Pole.

A doctor told Lonni that when patients are desperately ill, suffering great pain, or dying, they often call out for their mother. It is the call of the heart to go home again, to return to its source, to wrap its final breath in the memory of being loved. Love is the best memory of our wayward hearts. We are looking for what our heart already knows. The way back, whispers Benedict, is this way. Come follow and I will show you the way of hospitality.

one

The Taming of Hospitality

Catherine had never felt accepted. You know the kind of kid; you went to school with a few of them. It was as if she had been selected the very first day of kindergarten to be always on the outside. Maybe she was wearing mismatched mittens one day, or she still had peanut butter on her breath from breakfast. Maybe she wore the same shoes her sister wore last year. Father Dan never knew the reason for her being the social outcast she was. By the time he met her on retreat, she was firmly in place as the target for the teenaged sport of ridicule.

Without knowing the details, you can be sure that Catherine spent a lot of very tough nights growing up. She must have wondered if her life meant anything and wondered if anyone would ever listen to her. She probably did not dare hope that she would ever be loved. It is hard to imagine, if you've never been the one on the outside, what it can do to you. Just getting out of bed each morning becomes an act of courage.

On one of the worst nights of her life, Catherine called Mary Cummings, Father Dan's partner in retreat ministry for almost thirty years. She called Mary because once, when Catherine had dropped books and whatever else she was carrying, Mary stopped and helped. Mary extended the simplest of courtesies to this girl that had known only contempt. By taking a moment to look into her eyes, say a few words, and help in an awkward situation, Mary demonstrated to Catherine that she could be counted on to care. On the night when Catherine honestly did not know if she wanted to see another sunrise, she called Mary.

When we speak of hospitality we are always addressing issues of inclusion and exclusion. Each of us makes choices about who will and who will not be included in our lives. To make such choices is inevitable; we do not have time to be everyone's best friend. The reasons we include and exclude are very personal. You and I probably can't even say why we become close to some people and have no interest in getting to know, or include, others. We only know that we prefer some, and others are harder to like.

Issues of inclusion and exclusion, while personal, are not just personal. Our entire culture excludes many people. If you are in a wheelchair, for example, you are excluded because there are places you can't go. If you are very young, if you are very old, you are excluded. In high school you can be excluded if you don't wear the right shoes or listen to the right music. Women are excluded, as are people of color, and those who practice a religion different from our own.

In our idealism about American life the poor are always excluded; they are our embarrassing little American secret. The American dream has failed the one in six children living in poverty. These children will, most likely, grow up to a lifetime of exclusion. Somewhere, sometime, you were excluded. Remember what that was like. Some people live with the experience constantly.

There was a common saying in Germany just before the Nazi reign: "The human body contains a sufficient amount of fat to make seven cakes of soap, enough iron to make a medium-sized nail, a sufficient amount of phosporus for two thousand match-heads, enough sulfur to rid one person of fleas." The Nazi view of humanity reduced us to nothing more than the usefulness of our physical components, and when that was used up it was fine to cast aside the human being.

But you and I are much more than what we appear to be. We are more than what we do. We are more than a social or economic class. In the movie *Elephant Man*, actor John Merrick is chased through a train station and cornered in a bathroom by a mob who see only his deformity, his difference from them. He cries out, "I am not an animal. . . . I am a human being. . . ."

This is the sound of every single human heart. It is the cry we make against all that would make us less human, the cry of the darkest night of our lives, the cry of the abandoned and the misunderstood and the excluded. "I am not an animal. I am like you. I am human."

I am not a street person.
I am not a token of my race or creed.
I am not a statistic.
I am not a divorcée.
I am not an AIDS patient.
I am not a sex object.

I am not a laborer.

I am not an "at-risk" kid.

I have a mind. I have a heart. I have a soul. I dream. I feel. I care. I am a human being.

Hospitality has an inescapable moral dimension to it. It is not a mere social grace; it is a spiritual and ethical issue. It is an issue involving what it means to be human. All of our talk about hospitable openness doesn't mean anything as long as some people continue to be tossed aside.

In a 1982 report, one ethicist put it this way: "the opposite of cruelty is not simply freedom from the cruel relationship, it is hospitality." Hospitality puts an end to injustice. But calling hospitality a moral issue does not tell us the whole truth about hospitality either. A moral issue can become bogged down in legalisms, and hospitality is no legalistic ethical issue. It is instead a spiritual practice, a way of becoming more human, a way of understanding yourself. Hospitality is both the answer to modern alienation and injustice *and* a path to a deeper spirituality.

As a culture, we are frightened people living behind locked doors, fashioning our homes as reclusive retreats from what we believe is a hostile world that drains us of the energies we most cherish. The world at our gate is a fearsome thing. We lock the doors, click on the security system, put on headphones, and enter a place where we hope to be left to ourselves but always keep an ear listening for the sound of disturbance. It's no surprise that we are lonelier than ever before.

If thousands of people can be laughing with a friend, walking to work, or getting ready for an appointment at their desk when they are annihilated, how can we feel safe anywhere, anytime? We can't make light of this reality, but neither do we need to live in fear.

How do we keep from fearing the stranger? How do you and I keep looking into the eyes of the stranger and conjure up acceptance for him? In the days following the September 11 attacks on New York and Washington, you may recall a lot of people talking about their nervousness and growing suspicion with the dark-skinned stranger, the one who talks a bit Middle Eastern, the one who has been their neighbor.

A couple months after the attack we visited Ground Zero. A man who lived in Dublin, but who had worked very near the Twin Towers for twelve years, told us that he hated the people "who did this terrible thing," and he wept. Then, in the next breath he gazed up to heaven and said, "You see, we are all the children of God, made in his very own image, and that makes it unbearable. The hating has to stop. 'Tis sadder than words can say." 'Tis. And in the days that followed many sad things happened.

You may remember that in some instances the person with feared ethnic characteristics was removed from planes by passenger request, regardless of their innocence. People who were part of a community, who had been considered neighbors, suddenly became suspect, even if your kids went to school together and you bowled together on Tuesday night.

Two of the monks at St. Benedict Monastery are rather dark-skinned and would appear Middle Eastern to those who do not know their actual ancestry. Father Damien is Albanian; Brother Antony is from Puerto Rico. Often, they have been teased by their brother monks about looking like terrorists in their driver's license pictures. It had been good-natured teasing, but it is no longer funny.

Imagine the difficulty these men will have getting on a plane, or the discomfort they will cause others. Two of the biggest hearts on the planet, two of the greatest spirits, and if either of them sits beside you on

the taming of hospitality | 7

an airplane your heart will probably fall to your stomach and your pulse will race. You will want them removed; at the very least you will want them double-checked. You could not find two safer human beings if you scoured the universe, yet they are suddenly suspect because of skin color and ethnic features. The events of terrorism have created a new, dark filter through which we view the world.

We comfort ourselves by thinking, "But it isn't an unreasonable fear. Some awful things have happened and they have been done by men who look a certain way." Contrary to the comforting lies we tell each other, this kind of fear *is* unreasonable. Every person of Middle Eastern descent is not responsible for the big, awful thing that happened. Timothy McVeigh did not cause people to fear every white male, not unless you already thought white guys were dangerous.

The horror of September 11, 2001, did not create bigotry against Muslims; it incited existing bigotry. It fed a silently held bigotry already alive in a dark corner of our hearts. It uncapped a quietly seething suspicion.

It is easier to fear a whole group of people instead of giving one person a chance. It becomes easy to hate and to turn away from people we have vilified. To live courageously means giving up the fear and giving every single person a chance. "The home of the brave" is a wonderful ideal, but it is no easy thing to become. Brave people take a risk with the stranger. Brave people offer up their hearts, again, after they've pieced together the fragments of a broken heart. Brave people don't let themselves off the hook when something has gone wrong inside of them.

Fear is a thief. It will steal our peace of mind and that's a lot to lose. But it also hijacks relationships, keeping us sealed up in our plastic world with a fragile sense of security.

Being a people who fear the stranger, we have drained the life juices out of hospitality. The hospitality we explore here is not the same kind you will learn about from Martha Stewart. Benedictine hospitality is not about sipping tea and making bland talk with people who live next door or work with you. Hospitality is a lively, courageous, and convivial way of living that challenges our compulsion either to turn away or to turn inward and disconnect ourselves from others.

Hospitality is not optional to a well-balanced and healthy life. It meets the most basic need of the human being to be known and to know others. It addresses the core loneliness that we avoid with the bustle and haste of our hectic lives. There is a big loneliness at the center of every person. It is universal. There's a reason for the loneliness. It is meant to lead you somewhere. Even if you are unconscious of it, the big lonely is driving you homeward.

Hospitality has two meanings for most people today. It either refers to hotels or cruise ships, or it is connected to entertaining friends and family in the warmth of candlelight with gleaming silver and ivory lace. One model makes it an industry, thereby assigning some productive use to it and making it profitable. The other model relegates it to the domain of entertainment and housekeeping, generally considered women's work. Thus it has become safe and cozy, even productive, rather than revolutionary, risky, and world-rattling.

Benedictine hospitality does not allow us to turn people into a profit-making venture, nor are goodness and graciousness deemed suitable only for the cozy small world of our private homes and feminine natures. Benedict finds God in people. You can't ignore people when God is looking out their eyes at you. In the tiresome, the invalid, the rebellious, we are faced with God. It is our own failures to love that we have to deal with when we talk of hospitality.

Hospitality cuts through the sham of our excuses. Benedict is a realist about loving. He knows love comes only through effort and practice. It is costly. It is fatiguing. It is not some warm, fuzzy feeling Benedict wants us to conjure up; he wants the strength of respect and reverence to beat in the hearts of his monks.

When we are filled with prejudice, suspicion, anxiety, or jealousy, we have no room for welcoming, for listening or receiving. The monastic life allows the monk to empty himself of the darker impulse, not that he is ever completely rid of it, but he actively resists in the sharing of the table and the embracing of strangers.

Hospitality did not begin with Howard Johnson's and *Good Housekeeping*. Hospitality, as it has been practiced from ancient days, protected people from the dangers of traveling alone. In Saint Benedict's day there were no safe and cheap shelters for travelers. Along the way people could be brutalized, robbed, wounded, lost.

Monasteries saved lives when they opened their doors to strangers. It was not about comfort and entertainment—it was about saving lives. A little dramatic? Well, it seems that way today when we have a Marriott on every corner, shelters for the homeless and the battered, and hostels around the world.

This spirit of saving lives is still at the root of monastic hospitality. To receive others is to expose myself to all sorts of frightful dangers of attachment and rejection. Hospitality acknowledges the vulnerability of being human, both my humanity and that of the stranger. Travelers, too, (Benedict called them pilgrims), are prone to all sorts of dangers. On life's journey each of us is a pilgrim. We aren't sure where we came from and where we are going. We are vulnerable and we need each other.

Some of the most moving stories of hospitality have come out of the Holocaust. One Dutch woman, who now lives in a small Michigan town, told of growing up in a household that sheltered a Jewish family. All such stories are inspiring and remarkable, but hers was especially so because her parents kept the secret so well that their four children did not know a Jewish family was sheltered in their home. The parents risked everything to protect strangers, literal strangers, whose presence threatened them and their children.

This kind of sacrificial hospitality is almost more than we can imagine. We will probably never be called on to give ourselves for the sake of a stranger—but can we give some small part of ourselves to a stranger? We probably will never have to build a secret room in our homes to save the lives of people we don't know—but can we carve out a small place in our hearts for others? This is the true meaning of hospitality.

Monasteries are increasingly making room for strangers, by planning their lives to allow room for guests. This hospitality is included in the Benedictine rule, but it is also the current reality of monasteries. People are knocking on the door. People of all faiths or no faith at all are drawn to something about monasticism. The challenge for Benedictines is to preserve their monastic distinction, their way of life, while continuing to welcome the stranger. It is similar to the challenge you face as you attempt to keep time for yourself and your closest relationships while developing an open attitude.

The walking dead stand at the gates of the monastery. If life doesn't kill your wonder, it will at least wound your spirit. The monastic way is sometimes called the path of life, and life is what we seek. People go to the monastery in search of life. Today, Benedictines are not physically saving lives by their tradition, but they do continue to save lives. The spirit of monastic hospitality gives us something healing and rejuvenating. So, while practically speaking, hospitality has changed since Benedict's day, the lifesaving spirit of it has remained.

Those of us who don't live in monasteries have lost both the practice of hospitality itself as well as an open spirit that welcomes others. Not only our homes, but also we, like the monastery, need to become a place of solace and safety. Benedictine spirituality insists that if you want to be whole, you have to let the other in.

The missing virtue of our era has been turned into a social grace that neither disturbs nor transforms. That is not what Benedict meant when he shaped a way of life that would value at its deepest core, then and now, a life of hospitality.

Today, we take to ourselves only those we have met at work or in our neighborhood. We eat with our family. We lunch with our friends. If we ever include a stranger, it had better be a stranger that someone can vouch for. The outcast, the foreigner, the unacceptable person, these we avoid with a tight fear that chokes the life out of what it means to be hospitable.

You protest. There is very real danger in the stranger. Open the house and open a threat to my sleeping children? Open the door and violence enters. What about all the kooks with a knife? You read the countless horror stories with tragic endings. You aren't making all this stuff up, it is real and only a fool would ignore the dangers.

In this culture, is it possible to recover the gentle art of hospitality? Is there a way to enliven it, a way to recreate it so that personal safety is not at risk, but still the stranger is welcomed and honored? A lofty goal? Probably, but worth the effort we think. It is worthwhile for no other reason than this: When I consider the stranger I am faced with my worst fears. I can't deny that I am afraid and that I don't even always like people.

Many years ago Lonni was considering a vocational change that would put her, a fierce introvert, into constant contact with others. Lonni does not talk to strangers easily. She has a deep cynicism that prevents most people from getting too close. It was a service vocation, and she would have been unable to escape people.

The vocational counselor listened to her concerns, and then said with unhidden bewilderment, "I know you're sincere in pursuing this path, but I really don't understand what makes you think you'd be good at this—you don't even like people all that much." It was said with kindness and a twinkle in the counselor's eye. Hyperbole sometimes makes the point best. For Lonni, learning to like people would be the work of a lifetime.

Once you get over linking hospitality to the travel industry and dinner parties you still have to deal with that awkward reality of strangers. Hospitality involves accepting responsibility to care for the strangers, the ones at our gate, but also those a world away. The biggest obstacle to hospitality is not the state of the world. It is the state of our minds and hearts. It is the comfort we crave so badly that we will do almost anything for it.

Benedictine hospitality prevents us from living either desperately or indifferently. Hospitality requires not grand gestures, but open hearts. When I let a stranger into my heart, I let a new possibility approach me. When I reach past my own ideas, I begin to stretch myself open to the world, and this opening of my heart could change everything. That's pretty frightening stuff. You can't ever be the same if you start doing that kind of thing.

How we do this is an individual matter. It is the door of *my* heart that these strangers are knocking on.

Once you hear the sound at the door, you know a response is required. My response will be different from yours and different from a monk. Relating to others always involves the patterns you have learned in other relationships. Hospitality comes easily for those who have known mostly acceptance and love. For other people, it will come harder.

A friend told us a story from his recent illness:

> When I was very ill, it was necessary to receive frequent intravenous treatments, injections, blood tests, and many intrusive medical treatments. At first I had the courage for it, but day after day I lost courage, until the day a small Korean woman, the head nurse, walked into my hospital room after several failed attempts to find a vein. I glared at her, pushed her hand away, and said, "I can't take this anymore."
>
> She nodded and held my hand, and we sat in the quiet for a minute or so. Then, she said, "I just finished injecting medication into a permanent port in the belly of a twelve-year-old boy who will probably die before the year is over. I could not take what I do if it weren't for the fact that sometimes

what I do saves a life." I extended my arm and gave her my vein.

No, it is not easy to give your vein. Even when you know it is for your own good, you also know there's going to be pain involved. The things we'll do to avoid pain. There is a lot of pain that goes with relationships and from some of it, we never quite recover but, the pain you're carrying around, it can be used to save a life. It is not needless or pointless pain. No, you would not have volunteered for it. But it could save a life, and that's worth it.

Maybe you are one of the fortunate people who find hospitality easy. If so, you can probably look back to definite times you felt connected to others and well loved. If you have experienced abiding and strong relationships, hospitality comes more easily. One of us asked a student to write about a friendship she remembered:

> I remember my first loss of a friend, but it isn't the loss that has stayed with me, it is the friendship. My best friend Terry and I were seven. She lived next door, but next door was down the street a little

ways. You walked through a maze of brush, a maze carved out by my brother and his pals who liked to play fort in that brush. The brush was a jungle to the boys, but to us it was the enchanted forest where our friendship grew. Terry and I shared everything, our toys and books, our rooms and our families. We shared our dreams, too.

We promised that when we grew up, we would have houses next door to one another in the mountains we had seen in pictures. She would have a big barn for her horses; I would have a big library for my books. It was the summer of our seventh year and I was sure that, no matter what, we would be friends. I didn't see circumstances beyond our control approaching.

Her father was in the Coast Guard and he was being moved. No matter how much I wanted it, she could not take me with her and I could not keep her with me. Years passed and I have never seen Terry again. And while she hasn't told me a joke in fifteen years, the laughter remains. We haven't held hands to walk past the bully, but the strength lives on. We haven't raced and danced in our enchanted forest but life has seemed enchanted ever since. We never built those houses in the mountains, but I think of her when I see a mountain. When you have a friend, you have the best this life has to give.

A friendship like that will make you the kind of person who is able to be hospitable. Hospitality is born in us when we are well loved by God and by others. Hospitality is the overflowing of a heart that has to share what it has received. It takes a whole person to open up, it takes a secure person to be available, it takes a strong person to give yourself away.

It is possible to serve meals in a nursing home, to cook in a homeless shelter, or read stories to children at an inner-city library and never let others into your heart. It is possible to do the good thing and end up feeling satisfied with yourself and even just a bit superior. It is possible to do the good thing and not be changed for the better by it. Hospitality includes cooking the meal, and reading to the kid, but it demands that you let the people you are serving into your heart. Only in opening yourself wide to another are you transformed by the power of love.

If you are already thinking of ways to be more hospitable, just slow down. Do not worry just yet about opening up your door; focus on opening your heart. Do not worry about the time involved or how you can make it happen. Instead, look inside and see if you can find an empty space where you can let someone in.

Merely being nice to people does not fulfill the deep requirements of Benedictine hospitality. We must let the person stir us; we must connect. Benedictine hospitality will extract a cost from us, and it will tumble us into the magical realm of personal transformation.

Opening yourselves to the stranger is not equivalent to leaving your door unlocked and bringing strangers into your home. Hospitality does not mean you ignore obvious threats to personal safety. Hospitality means bringing strangers into your heart, which may or may not result in inviting strangers to the table. Do not harden your heart against suffering. Widen your boundaries to include those who are not like you. When monks open up their monastery, they are making a place for someone who is not one of them. You and me, we are the strangers at the door of the monastery.

We take our rumbling fears and hopes, our silent regrets, our dumb ideas, and our half-formed self with us to the monastery. We are complicated strangers, not always easy to love strangers. One friend of the monastery remembers going there late one afternoon. It was one of those days. You know the kind. The world is spinning too fast and your soul is too slow. One of those days when someone has ripped off the last chunk of you and there's nothing left.

She was new to the monastery. She didn't know the schedule, when the monks prayed, when they ate meals. She would have been more considerate of the pattern of their life together, but she didn't know. Because of this, she showed up that stormy, spring afternoon just as the monks were finishing Vespers and readying for dinner. She didn't call first. She just aimed her car toward the monastery, the only place in the world that seemed safe.

The retreat house was jammed with teenagers on retreat. Father Dan and the staff were enormously occupied with the teens. When she arrived, she parked her car and started walking, nearly blind with tears. She walked down to the pond and walked back. She stood at the fence and watched the cows.

"I'm not sure what I was doing there or what I expected," she remembers. "I knew it was a safe place.

I just felt that if I got there, somehow I would be better for it. I felt that I'd get help in handling the tangle of feelings and painful emotions.

"I got out of my car and walked around a little. There are several buildings on the monastery grounds. The monastery is across the driveway from the retreat house. I tried not to give in to the tears that burned my eyes, but I wasn't succeeding. I was friends with one of the monks and maybe I thought he'd materialize out of thin air, but he was off praying and dining with his brother monks."

She didn't see the storm gathering over her head. She remained at the fence, watching the cows, silent, waiting for something she could not name. She continues,

A hand descended on my shoulder and I turned to look into the smiling, concerned face of Father Dan. He didn't know me well. We'd met only a time or two after mass. His eyes quickly took in my tear-stained face, and he asked without prelude if I would like him to fetch my friend or did I want to be alone?

The man had fifty teenagers in the retreat house doing God only knows what, as he stood at the edge of the cow pasture with me. I replied that I wasn't sure. Not a particularly helpful response to his question. He said, "Please, come inside then," and motioned toward the retreat house. On the way inside I noticed large threatening clouds gathering in the evening sky. Not only was he concerned about what I was feeling, he wanted to get me out of the elements, too.

Once inside, he put a cup of hot chocolate in my hand and said, "The monks are having dinner. Can I get you something to eat? We have pizza here at the retreat house. Or, I could get you a beer." His voice was edged with anxiety. He offered me everything short of a pot roast. He wanted to ease the pain.

He must have recognized that he was overwhelming me a bit because he fell silent, sat with me, and allowed me to collect myself. Then I told him I would like to talk to my friend. He went over to the monastery, found the monk, and delivered him to my side.

The interruption of the retreat program and the monastic day was not welcome. Father Dan is no different from any of us that way. He does not look forward to having his plans disrupted and having to deal with an additional problem.

His lifetime of monastic formation, however, prevented him from ignoring the woman. He felt the same frustration anyone would feel when faced with such a situation, but he also knows that moments like these hold the potential for holy presence—and that's not something to hide from. When such a moment presents itself, you run toward it and expect that God will show up.

The Benedictine is not merely gracious; he is available. He does not observe human pain from a distance; he gets up to his elbows in it. He can wait with you while you try to make words. There is a deep, open place in his heart where others can come and go. This is Benedictine hospitality. He does not have to attach himself to every person who passes through this open heart of his, however; he can love them at the moment and let them go on.

We are going to have moments when we want no one to cross the threshold of our lives. We are going to experience, at our best, the urge to bolt and run. It helps to know that this happens to the most caring of persons; it happens to the monk. Hospitality calls us to push past those feelings and extend ourselves.

Hospitality enables you to joyfully make room for another inside your open heart. It stretches the brittle, tight heart. A closed-up heart can never relax, never allow you to enjoy another, to play, to relish the unguarded moment of surprise. It is always waiting for the other person to strike.

Only the secure person can live with an open heart. To do so is a whole lot braver than it sounds. You become susceptible to all sorts of human oddities and strangeness. You will be misunderstood. You will be rejected. Doubts you could otherwise avoid, will circle your feet. You have to resolve the issue of whether or not the universe is a safe place. Only the brave keep the door ajar.

A brave heart eventually shines with the divine presence; like God they are free, they are welcoming and accepting, they are strong, yet gentle. They are wondrously available. Yes, it will be costly. People will enter your heart and your life; they will become precious to you and then they will leave. An open heart will be broken. This is all undeniable.

But, by remaining open we learn about ourselves and we grow in ways we'd never otherwise grow. We discover why it is hard for us to trust and love. We encounter the broken places we have ignored; we listen to the voices of our deepest longings to connect. We pay attention to distinctions. We learn the sound of a malicious lie and learn to discern it from the whisper of a frightened one. Discernment, a vital element in wisdom, grows in those who remain open despite the high cost.

As the practice of hospitality increases our wisdom and openness, we tend to become more aware of the deeper implications of hospitality. We come to recognize that the need for hospitality goes deeper than we originally realized. Pursuing a life of hospitality will eventually make you realize its social and moral implications. What you do, as one person, to receive others does matter. Hospitality, however, involves us not only as individuals, but also as our entire culture. In a culture that excludes others, prejudice and hatred are common. Prejudice has deeper effects, in addition to simply causing people to exclude others: It is at the root of a hostility that is cruel and violent.

We have made great strides in understanding one another better, but there will be prejudice until you and I deal with our prejudice. There will be sexism until we rip up its roots in our own hearts. Until we take people of other races into our hearts we will not recognize "them" as real human beings. Until we have loved a gay person we will fear a gay person. Until we get to know someone who practices a religion different than our own, our differences will divide us. The walls only come down when the labels are changed into human faces.

Recently, Lonni's granddaughter Gina has been going through what the pediatrician says is a normal stage of development for a child of four. Gina has become frightened of sleeping. The world she knows changes when she sleeps. The cute little stuffed bear at the foot of her bed growls in the night and nibbles on her toes. The whirl of her ceiling fan is comforting when sunlight streams through the windows, but at night it casts shadows that transform the security of her room into a threatening jungle.

Gina copes with the trauma of the night by developing a complicated set of rituals that eases her away from the people she loves into the mystery of the night she faces alone. Bedtime is important because it helps us learn to face our fears and deal with the unknown. Rituals such as taking the last drink of water, reading five books, and leaving the door open three—not two, not four, but three—inches, gives the child some sense of control over this frightening thing.

The most important ritual for Gina is having someone sit at the edge of her bed while she falls asleep. She will cease the continual requests to go to the bathroom one more time, or get another tissue, or rearrange a shelf of books, if someone simply sits with her, puts a comforting hand on hers, and stays with her in the night for a few minutes.

What we need as we take steps toward the frightening idea of hospitality is someone to sit with us until it feels more comfortable. We don't need to be judged or scolded for our unsettled feelings and fears. We need a companion in the darkness. Benedict and his monks are our companions in this unknown region. We will not whistle in the dark and pretend to be unafraid, and we will not deny the inherent dangers. Acknowledging fear, facing fear, and sitting with it, this is a spiritual approach to hospitality.

Night prayer is the way the monks go into the depths of mystery. Night is a sacred time of silence at a monastery. Each monk goes bravely into the night silence alone, and yet his brothers accompany him. If facing the possibility of hospitality can be compared to entering the unknown mystery of night, there is no better companion for the journey into the night than the monk. He knows this region. He has been there. He won't be easily startled by what rattles and chills the night.

In monasticism, the night is a holy time. God is experienced in the darkness in a way that is unique to darkness. And God in the dark makes the frightful thing less so. Fear chokes out love. We don't become people of love unless we have faced our fears. This doesn't always mean resolution. Overcoming fears can be the work of a lifetime.

Hospitality is the way we learn to really love; it is the way out of our own brooding fears and broken hearts. Benedictine hospitality is a far cry from the tame social grace we have come to call hospitality. Hospitality feels risky, but it is the most ordinary of human experiences. In a less complicated world, less painful world, we would not be discussing *how* to open up; we would simply do it.

It is not a comforting thing for the future or our race that we discuss simple human relations as if we are doing quantum physics. Just as a person with a healthy digestive system doesn't talk about it, people with healthy relationships don't make a fuss over it, they just live a certain way. When our lives are working and our spirits are alive, we are mostly unaware of ourselves.

That doesn't mean our interest in how to be more loving and accepting is sick. The interest is normal and healthy, but there is a soul sickness that provokes the discussion. We are not as well adjusted as we think we are. The widespread talk of spirituality in our culture is not encouraging news about the state of our spirits. And this is the place where we must begin. We must go into the places inside of us we avoid. We must take a deep breath, and take a hand, and be brave. Hospitality does not require a new cookbook and tea set. It requires what we used to call conversion.

two

Hospitality Begins Inside

*I*n considering the meaning and ways of hospitality, we are looking for a first step in a new direction. It's natural. It's something we human beings need: a first thing to do, followed by another thing, and then another. How do you begin? It is important to understand that we aren't offering ten easy steps to hospitality. That is not how spiritual practices work.

Well, then, how do spiritual practices work? A spiritual practice is an action intended to make a change or adjustment in the deepest realm of the self. A spiritual practice is a thing we do that opens a door. It might be meditation or prayer. It could be serving the poor. Stripping life of what is unessential and practicing simplicity—that is a spiritual practice. The spiritual practice creates a possibility or opportunity, but the change itself is more gift than effort. The spiritual practice puts us into a receiving place where we are open to the something more that we call God. You can set your will to be more open to others, but your heart still has to stretch gradually.

This description is hard to wrap the mind around when so much of contemporary culture approaches spirituality from a self-help angle. American spirituality is basically consumer spirituality. God is a product with incredible benefits. God helps us live well, live healthfully, be prosperous and emotionally strong. God is like a great motivational speaker or talk show host who offers a banquet of options for successful spirituality. You look over the banquet table and select what appeals to you.

We are caught up in what is probably the most immature attempt at spirituality humanity has ever seen. It is tragically and poignantly adolescent, with the deep emotion and angst that goes with adolescence. It is a spirituality that seeks improvement for life—a better me, a better relationship—but it does not seek God and it does not move us toward others. It just keeps us running on the treadmill of our little egocentric worlds.

We are accustomed to easy answers. Hospitality is not an easy answer. It requires that we take a chance and we change. It requires us to grow. The moment we engage with another person everything gets messy. Our time becomes not quite our own; we can count on others interrupting us. We become subject to a whole hoard of emotional dangers.

Because hospitality always involves giving something of ourselves to others, it is a spiritual practice. Spirituality is about relationship. When you and I become confused about the meaning of spirituality, remembering that spirituality is about relationship will bring us back to the basics. Relationships.

If you receive many mail order catalogs, you have noticed that common household items and clothing are now sold with a spiritual promise. Turn on your soothing music, wrap up in your cotton robe and curl up beneath a silk-and-wool afghan, light a candle, and plug in your flowing fountain. The ads suggest that you should now be feeling spiritual. And it cost you only a couple hundred dollars.

What we want in spirituality today is comfort. Tom Waite and Kathleen Brennan wrote a song called "Chocolate Jesus." It's about wanting a Jesus that tastes good, gives you the comforts of sweets and fast food, and makes you feel good inside.

> Well it's got to be a chocolate Jesus
> Good enough for me
> Got to be a chocolate Jesus
> Good enough for me
> Well it's got to be a chocolate Jesus
> Make me feel good inside
> Got to be a chocolate Jesus
> Keep me satisfied (Jaima Music)

Americans want chocolate spirituality that soothes and feels good. We think it is "good enough for me," but it isn't, it's not good enough for anyone. Genuine spirituality is not cozy, and seldom makes you comfortable. It challenges, disturbs, unsettles, and leaves you feeling like someone is at the center of your existence on a major remodeling mission. While affirming how wonderful you are, better than you really know, spirituality is also meant to change you. If it doesn't, it is something less than spirituality.

This tendency of ours to seek out comfort should tell us something about ourselves. We lack. We need.

We sense something is not quite right. But Chocolate Jesus and Chicken Soup don't help the problem. We need stronger medicine for our sickly souls. We need a transforming, shake-you-to-the-soles-of-your-feet kind of remedy. We need transforming Love.

You want to be open, you want to let others into your life—what do you do? Whatever plan you devise, one thing is undeniable: such a change starts within. It begins with who you are and who you are becoming. It is a spiritual journey.

We recently received an e-mail from a student in Indonesia who had read books we have authored. In his correspondence he said very gracious things and at the end he wrote, "May I know you better?"

Here is the core of hospitality: May I know you better? Will you come closer, please? No, it will not be easy, but make no mistake about it, your life depends on this saving stranger coming to you and stretching your tight little heart.

Hospitality is a personal response to your own need to connect with other people. This need is at the core of what it means to be human. Your entire humanity, your identity itself is wrapped up in your need to connect. The real question is not how dangerous that stranger is. The real question is how dangerous will I become if I don't learn to be more open?

Choosing against hospitality means you will eventually lock your heart away from others and grow cold and hard inside. You cannot take seriously the spiritual practice of hospitality and remain as you are. If you are serious about it, nothing will ever be the same again.

Recently, the J. R. R. Tolkien classic, *The Lord of the Rings,* has gained popularity as a movie based on the books. The books are the story of one person's (well, one hobbit's) resistance to evil and his mission in life to stop the invasion of evil. Along the way he finds companions and they, too, are forced to make decisions about the kind of people they will be and what they will spend their lives for.

The hobbit is an interesting character because he is considered by most to be not quite human, a "halfling," part human, part animal (he is small and has animal-like feet which never require shoes or boots). He does not try to be anything other than what he is, he lives at peace with this in-between state of his, and he does what he is given to do. The message is a simple one. We are, none of us, as human as we might be. We are all still part animal. This mixed bag is our reality, but it does not prevent us from doing the great and good things we are given to do.

At one point the hobbit sets out to fight evil on his own but discovers in the movie that he cannot get rid of his companions. They are part of whatever plan exists in our universe. They are part of the struggle against not only the darkness in our universe, but the darkness inside as well. We are in this together.

Hospitality, rather than being something you achieve, is something you enter. It is an adventure that takes you where you never dreamed of going. It is not something you do, as much as it is someone you become. You try and you fail. You try again. You make room for one person at a time, you give one chance at a time, and each of these choices of the heart stretches your ability to receive others. This is how we grow more hospitable—by welcoming one person when the opportunity is given to you.

The other day over lunch the two of us overheard an interesting conversation. Two couples, both in their forties, were discussing matters such as Sunday school classes and how to talk to others about faith. In the middle of the conversation one man in the group told the story of going to a huge march in Washington several years ago with a million other men, all in the name of Christian faith. He talked about how their walking route was "littered with the homeless and people begging." One of his friends obviously was struggling with his feeling that they should have stopped to help these people. The others in the group discouraged him from such thoughts by saying, "Hey, they've made their choice. No one is making them do this. They could get a job."

In their conversation they wondered about what to do in these situations. As they talked, a fear surfaced.

"Yeah, we know we're supposed to help people, but what if this is what they do for a living? I mean, what if they go drive a Mercedes home at the end of the day?"

Maybe they really are not poor. Maybe they are ripping me off. They are getting what they deserve. They have made their own choices. There are programs to help people like them. I am not doing them a favor if I give them a handout. I am not going to contribute to their condition.

We have all heard that voice rattling around in our heads. These people were wrestling with the same kinds of things you and I leave unsaid day after day.

There are no easy answers. Benedict offers none except that we must be open to others, *especially*, he says, the poor and the outcast. Benedict was Christian and so Jesus was his model for how to treat the poor.

Jesus told his followers: If you ignore them, you ignore me. If you feed them, you feed me. So, Benedict tells his monks, receive every person as if you are receiving Christ himself.

The foursome appeared to be honestly grappling with the issue; you could not doubt their sincerity. They wrestle with these issues because they are people of faith and Jesus gave Christians only one option. You help when you can help. Give what you have. The resolution to the big problem is somehow, mysteriously, wrapped up in this uniquely Christian notion that Jesus is in the poor. When we turn away from the poor, we lose Jesus and we lose ourselves.

We can't know how our behavior changes everything, but it does. We call that faith. It was not Washington's homeless those good Christian men walked past, it was Jesus. Daily, Benedict tells his monks, you and I will encounter Jesus. You will stroll right past him if you aren't careful. Instead, look closer, look in the person's eyes, search for that spark of light, and let yourself be open to the possibility of God coming to you in the stranger.

In most situations we get ourselves into trouble by what we do: adultery, lying, stealing, jealousy, and so on. Not so in hospitality: Our error comes through what we fail to do. When it comes to hospitality we become less by what we omit doing. Every time we turn away we drop a little of our humanity.

The point is not even whether or not you change the world by putting a dollar in the hand of one hungry person. The point is that you be open. Anyone can give a few dollars today, anyone can take someone for a cup of coffee, anyone can drop a blanket around someone's shoulders.

These are little acts, to be sure, but little acts push at the great big darkness, the darkness that is so huge we feel helpless and so we do nothing and try to make ourselves feel good about it. This is a heart problem. We don't lack resources or opportunity, we lack heart. You can't fix the problem of world hunger. Well, no, of course you can't. Where did you ever get the idea you were supposed to? But you can help the single mother feed her kids, and you can help the old guy whose Social Security check won't come for another week.

You and I, we can help the one in our path. That is enough. Try to get this straight, that really is enough.

Imagine that all of life is a great symphony. You play the violin. That is what you are good at, it is what you love, it is what you were made to do. So play it. Become really good at playing your notes, and just your sound can be incredible, but you will not be the whole symphony. The symphony requires all the other musicians.

But the violinist must play her notes if the symphony is to be the wonder it is and is supposed to be. She is neither the whole symphony nor insignificant.

We read books, listen to speakers, talk to the older and wiser, hoping that they will offer some method, some path toward becoming more loving. We want someone to give us the next step. Hospitality is not a self-improvement goal to be achieved, such as giving up smoking. Hospitality is not about what you do, it is about who you are becoming. You can press the linens, invite the homeless, and serve the ham. And unless you are willing to let people into your locked-up secret place you will remain alone and so will they.

This becoming tends to be subtle rather than startling. It starts with a choice to begin. That is how all change starts: You decide it is time to change.

Somewhere, sometime you will be presented with a choice. You can listen to the old woman and be ten minutes late for your meeting or you can rush her, maybe even ignore her—and be admirably prompt. You can put down the phone and listen to your co-worker talk for a minute. You can shut off the radio and play checkers with your child. A healthy practice of hospitality means finding a healthy balance. It is about priorities as well as the state of your heart. How much do people matter? How important is it to make room for others?

Just the other day Father Dan was telling a handy-man about the needs of one special teenager who has been on retreat a couple of times. "She's a wonderful girl," he told the handyman. "I'm not sure what her physical impairment is, but she is weaker on one side than the other." He instructed the handyman to install handrails in the bathroom and shower of the room where the girl would be staying. One girl. Thousands of teens will make a retreat at the monastery this year, but Dan made room for one girl.

That is where it starts. You make room in your heart, room in your life, room in the moment for one person, with no strings attached.

All your life someone has been reminding you not to talk to strangers. All of these well-meaning people only wanted to protect you when you were a child. You are not a child any longer; it is time for you to determine how you will respond to the strangers among us. What is dangerous to the child is not dangerous to an adult. You drive a car now. You live away from home. You use knives to chop vegetables. You drink a scotch and water. Why do we remain locked up in our fear of strangers?

Sharon, a thirty-something-year-old woman from a small midwestern town, was on a committee formed to consider establishing a homeless center in conjunction with an established center in a nearby troubled city. The inner-city shelter housed more men each night than they could handle. In someone's will, the shelter had been given a large, well-built home in Sharon's quiet little town. The plan was to bus the extra men to that home each night and then back to the streets of the city the next day after breakfast. Sharon joined the committee because she assumed they would be helping implement the plans.

Imagine how surprised she was to discover that the committee's actual goal was to prevent the homeless shelter from carrying out its plan. It was her first exposure to, "Yes, they need help, but not in our neighborhood," and "Our streets won't be safe with those people here," and "Homeless people are always a little nuts, you know."

Sharon knew she could not turn around the attitude of the committee. She chose to inform the shelter of the committee's true intention. She held out no hopes that her decision to inform would make a difference—and she was right. Ultimately the shelter sold the house and used the money to purchase and restore a building in the city. She knew it was a better plan than the original one, but she remained profoundly disturbed by what she had heard.

"It was such an awful thing they were doing to people they don't know. I'm not saying I never feel prejudice—but they would not even give the homeless a chance." The others ostracized Sharon, including several who went to church with her. To this day there are people who still call her "that woman." However, Sharon has continued to grow and let her heart be open to others. She lost friends, but she gained an open heart.

Hospitality means sharing. What a wildly quaint idea. We reserve the word *sharing* for toddlers these days. Hospitality allows us to grow into the human family and share space, share material, resources, and ourselves. The other option is to remain locked up in our little neighborhoods, frightened that someone different might sneak in. When I begin to realize that I am one among many, I begin to realize that someone else is real. Someone else has a right to space, too. Someone else has needs. Someone else has as much right to be here as I do. I am not more. I am not less. I am part of it all.

The work of opening up to others can be challenging. For most, there are more than a few personal barriers to overcome. We fear bonding and we fear detachment, and we seldom know how to strike a healthy balance between them. Growing more open is easier if we don't understand these twin realities as polar opposites. The need to belong and the need to be alone are both normal and do not exclude the other.

There are other problems: We may bond too quickly and too possessively. We may smother others with what we want to give them. No matter how much we want to know someone better and be present to him or her, we must not be obsessive and overwhelming. We need to stand back and let people find their way to our open hearts.

Brenda once attempted to develop a close friend-ship with a woman who prided herself on being "open and honest" with everyone. She told Lonni the story.

"Her idea of honesty was brutal. She said things like, 'You're much smarter than your wife. Why are you married to such a dimwit?' Or, 'Your father died because he smoked three packs of cigarettes a day.'

"She immediately wanted into your psyche, she wanted instant access to all your deepest regions and would get very upset when people didn't 'open up' to her. She considered it a deep fault. She was so bent on pushing you into being open and honest, that you didn't want her nearby."

Brenda watched her friend push away person after person, all the while blaming the others. It came to a head when a neighbor of Brenda's was hospitalized with a nervous breakdown, and her three children needed care and supervision.

"She was the first one to volunteer her help and sup-port. I admired that. When it came time for her to stay overnight with the children (their father worked nights) she asked me to drive her because her car was in the shop. We arrived just as the children's father was getting ready for work. After a couple minutes of small talk my friend said, 'What your wife needs is more love from you. You've failed as a husband or she wouldn't be in the hospital.' The young man was devastated. Those who knew the history knew the woman had been engaged in a struggle for her emotional health since her teens."

Brenda was furious with her friend. She could not believe that even this woman would say such a thing. Brenda decided she would also stay the night with the children. After the children were in bed she tried to talk about what had happened.

"As soon as I brought it up she left the room to make tea. I brought it up again and she became angry. She said that no one understood this was her gift and God had given her the responsibility of speaking the hard truth."

The friendship faded slowly, Brenda remembers. "If that was a gift of God, it was one I didn't understand, one that seemed unusually cruel and selfish. I tried to find the better part of her and that was easy; there was a lot to like. But in the moments when she turned on a person, it was so fierce. I chose not to put myself through that over and over again. What I learned in that relationship was to honor myself and make better choices in my relationships. I could have remained friends with her, but it was too costly to my peace of mind. I tried the best I knew, and then I allowed the relationship to die."

Part of the internal work hospitality requires is setting boundaries. You do no one a favor if you allow people to involve you in destructive behaviors. You have to figure out for yourself when this is happening. It is a matter of trusting yourself.

You can be accepting with people without trying to make everyone your best friend. It is not even healthy to try to be intimate with everyone. We will address this more later when we discuss intimacy in more detail. For now, keep in mind that hospitality requires a healthy set of personal boundaries you do not allow others to violate.

The paradox of relationship is that we will never achieve any better relationship with anyone else than we have achieved with ourselves. If you genuinely open up to others you will be unable to ignore all the stirrings inside of you, all the unresolved questions, and all the still-weeping wounds. You will be forced to look deeper into yourself. Others help us understand ourselves in all the annoyance, bewilderment, and companionship of relationship.

There is a kind of gentle hospitality with the self that most of us fail to practice. You know that moment you look in a mirror and see a stranger staring out those eyes? We don't accept the stranger within. We dread the regions of ourselves we don't understand. By learning to value the otherliness of the actual stranger, we honor the mystery within us, too.

The stranger in your house is not just yourself, it is your teenager or spouse or brother. Not only is there a stranger in your skin, there are several in your home too. The essence of hospitality is receiving the stranger while letting them remain a stranger. By letting the stranger into our "dwelling" (not necessarily a physical structure), we let them into our emotional and spiritual space. We welcome them to be heard and understood, we accept what they choose to reveal of themselves, and we accept them if they reveal little or nothing.

We've all been shocked by some hidden aspect of someone we have known and loved, or by some part of ourselves that suddenly reveals itself. It can be disturbing, yet we see the person in a new light, we pay closer attention, we ask questions, we cease taking them for granted and assuming we have mined the depths.

There is a value in the unknowing between people. Extending hospitality to the people we know means that we allow them freedom to make mistakes. It means we give them room to be who they are, rather than who we want them to be.

The mystery of the other is a reflection of God's mystery as well. God is ultimately the stranger who comes to us, the stranger within, the stranger who intrudes with her neediness and her hurting. God is the stranger we never quite understand.

Lonni remembers going to Father Dan when she was very disturbed over the behavior of a mutual acquaintance. She was surprised to learn that Dan had also struggled to understand and accept that particular individual. Dan's monastic training meant he tried extra hard to listen between the lines, he tried extra hard to find the good in this person even when the person was being a jerk. When asked for the secret to his patience, Dan shrugged his shoulders and said, "There's no secret to it, you just keep trying to understand."

We need patience, with others and with ourselves, if we are going to live hospitable lives. If we are impatient we invade other people and violate their sacred rights. Patience allows others to approach us as they feel welcome. Patience gives space. We become receptive to new ideas, to good criticism, to encouragement, to change.

A teenager told us how she discovered her own lack of patience. She was babysitting for the children across the street. Michael, a boy of three, resisted even what was good for him. He did not want to eat. He did not want to sleep. He did not want to share with his sister. He did not want a bath. He did not want her to put his pajamas on over his head; he wanted them pulled up over his feet. She knew there is nothing unusual about a strong-willed toddler, so her reaction to Michael surprised her.

"I wanted to hurl him out a window," she remembers. "I wanted to force the food down his throat and I wanted to tie him to his bed. The entire evening this terrible sense of violence was just under the surface. I had no patience for the child, none at all." The girl said when she talked to her mother, she realized that it was a control issue. Her inability to control the child or bend him to her will broke whatever reserves of patience she had. "Impatience is the offspring of the need to control," writes James Connor in his book

Silent Fire: Bringing the Spirituality of Silence to Everyday Life.

Hospitality may involve a major change of attitude and lifestyle for you, or it may be that you are already growing more open to others. But either way you will sometimes find it easy to welcome others, while at other times you will fight for every ounce of acceptance you offer. A battle to accept someone can seem like a struggle with no real value. Remind yourself that the struggle matters—it is making you stronger.

We know a woman who has a sculpture of a horse in the grips of an exerting struggle. It is a stunning sculpture: The dark form of the horse almost writhes in the agony of some huge unknown effort. Even after looking at it for hours, you cannot determine if the horse is falling down or getting up. You only see the exertion. Our friend says she changes her mind from day to day as to whether the horse is getting up or falling down. She says it seems to depend on what she is feeling that day. When she mentioned this to the artist, he said, "You know, it doesn't matter if the horse is falling down or getting up. What matters is it keeps trying."

In our relationships with others what matters is that we keep trying. There is a place inside that you must first open, before you open your door. Some days it will be hard to do that, other days it will be easier. What matters is that you keep trying.

three

Welcoming the Other

e was from Saudi Arabia, and if he sat next to you on a bus he'd make you nervous. But Lonni didn't meet him on a bus. She met him, his wife, and their two children while working as a volunteer at a refugee center, in a program run by the monastery that involves service projects by teens and adults. This particular project was slated to last only a few days, possibly a week.

Lonni was painting rooms the day she met him. He had just returned from a visit to the library, he told her. They talked a little. She noticed that his English was poor. They exchanged names, and he told her the name of his wife and his children, one boy, one girl, both under six.

He told her they were from Pakistan. He asked why she was painting rooms at the shelter and how she knew all the teenagers with her. She noticed that he listened to her words carefully. Sometimes he asked her to repeat something, and sometimes he repeated what she had said and asked if he had gotten it right. The conversation lasted twenty minutes or so; then he joined his family, and Lonni returned to painting.

The next day he sought out Lonni while she worked on another floor. Would she go with him to meet his family, he asked. He had told his wife about her and he thought his wife missed having a woman to talk with.

Lonni remembers her feelings. "He was very different than any person I had known. He was Muslim. I was Christian. My head buzzed with everything I had ever heard about Muslims, especially Muslim men."

But she liked his wife immediately. She had a wide smile and a soft voice. She had been in medical school and hoped to return some day. She was an intelligent woman trying to make the best of a terrible situation. Lonni remembers noticing the loving warmth that passed between the couple in small gestures, glances, and smiles. Their behavior was different than she expected and she was touched by it. Their children were delightful—nothing like children she expected to find in a refugee center.

The father asked the children to tell her something about a museum they had visited a few days before. They each did, carefully and slowly. The wife asked if the children were using the words correctly. They were, remarkably so, Lonni replied, and the parents beamed with pride.

That night, she wondered about the mysterious man and his family as she tried to sleep. She thought of all the stereotypes she carried around about Muslim families. It was disturbing to have the stereotypes so blatantly revealed. Still, she reminded herself, the man was a mystery. She didn't know the stories of the refugees, but she knew they were often fleeing for their lives. What had he done? That question lingered in her mind, too.

Mystery surrounds all human relationships but especially a relationship with a stranger. He was clearly accustomed to holding power. He carried himself like royalty, as did his whole family. The thing she could not understand, however, was his cheerfulness. She had spent very little time with him, but still, he had been cheerful without exception. There he was, dislocated from the only life he had ever known, and the man bubbled with hope and optimism.

"I went home that evening wondering about his motivations, asking myself what it was he wanted from me. He made me feel uneasy, not because of anything he did but because he was very different from any other person I had ever known. I thought Muslims disliked Christians. I thought Muslim men did not like or respect women. He had exploded the preconceptions of my clenched little heart in only a few hours," she remembers.

The next day he was waiting when she pulled into the parking lot with a van of teenagers. He asked if they could speak in private. They walked next door and sat on the steps of the church. There, he told her his story. He was a political refugee. His crime was resistance to what he considered rigid and evil political systems. He had been involved in lawmaking. He came from a prosperous family that owned more than one house. He talked of moving his bride into a twenty-four-room house when they married.

"It breaks my heart that she is making a home of a little room now," he said, lifting his eyes toward the center. "Her courage is so big that I will do all to give her a better life now." He was not sure how long he would be in America; there were rumors that they would soon be moved to Canada. He understood his present situation to be an opportunity, a gift of God. It was not a tragedy. He expected their life would be better, his children better, because they would grow up in the Western world.

He was at peace despite having left everything he had ever known. Despite being marked for assassination. Despite facing changes that would leave most people staggering, bitter, and frightened, he was at peace.

He told her that Allah had sent her to his family to teach them "better English." He had watched her, he said, and noticed that she worked hard, treated others kindly. He was not sure, but he thought her English was above average. Would she teach him, and his family, about America? Would she help them improve their English?

"There is nothing to give you in return but we will give gratitude," he said.

She did not know what to say. She was not sure such a thing would be allowed by the center. They were very protective of the residents. She told him she would need permission from the program director.

"I didn't agree and that disappointed him. My real problem was not whether or not I would be allowed to help. He still made me uneasy. I could not imagine having anything to offer them either. They were so different. They made me hugely uncomfortable."

Lonni had become a good friend of the monks by this time. Observing their lives, listening to them talk, reading St. Benedict, she was sure that helping them was the right thing to do. But it was also the difficult thing to do. She did not realize until she talked to the program director just how difficult.

Yes, she could "tutor" the family, the director said, but she could not tell them her full name, where she was from, or discuss her family. "Do not give them your phone number," the director ordered, "or your address." They could not tell her anymore about themselves than they had already (and the director was *not* pleased with what they had already revealed). She said that when the family was relocated to their final destination, there could be no more contact between them.

Strengthened by her blossoming understanding of Benedictine hospitality, Lonni hesitatingly agreed to help the family. For the next six weeks she spent two afternoons a week with the Muslim family.

"Before long I started looking forward to our time together. The tutoring sessions were nothing like I expected. We talked and we read newspapers together, we went to movies or museums. We visited the zoo. I read book excerpts to them sometimes. I told them stories of growing up in Middle America and being Catholic.

Lonni shed her assumptions about Muslims in those weeks, not because she is by nature without prejudice, but because the mysterious Muslim now had a face, a laughing face with bright, dark eyes and a friendly welcome for her. She had taken on the task of teaching them about American culture, but they were doing something much more important for her. They were dismantling her fears and prejudices.

She remembers taking the children to see a Disney movie, leaving the parents to some rare time by themselves. The children sat on either side of her and she explained the movie. She knew they did not understand all her words but they laughed a lot and bounced to the music and ate bags of popcorn and drank gallons of lemonade. At one point during the movie the little girl rested her head sleepily on Lonni's shoulder and smiled up at her in the dim lights.

"It was such a universal gesture of trust. My own children had done that hundreds of time. It said, 'I trust you, and I feel safe and loved with you.'"

On the way home that day she taught them to sing "The Wheels on the Bus," and when she left them, they were teaching it to their parents and they were all laughing.

She showed up two days later and they were gone. The director explained that they had started their new life. She handed over a piece of blue scrap paper, folded in half. It said: "Thank you for considerations to us. You are a good woman and Christian. May Allah be with you all the days of your life and reward you for kindness to strangers."

Lonni was sure that the man was keeping his word and "giving gratitude." She wished she could tell him that they had already given her so much more. They had opened up a place inside of her, and they had banished some particularly fearsome things from her heart. They had taught her to love better.

"I felt the loss of my new friends deeply," Lonni says. "I still think of them sometimes and pray they are safe, happy, and free. They are the face of the Muslim faith for me."

Several years ago there was a popular song by Joan Osborne titled "One of Us." It asked, "What if God was one of us, just a stranger on the bus, trying to make his way home?" That is what Christians believe Jesus showed us about God, that God is one of us and is with us as we try to get home. God came to us to teach us how to live and how to love. One of the things he said, "Whatever you do to the least of my brothers and sisters, you do to me," means that God *is* the stranger on the bus. We are all strangers on the bus of this world trying to make our way home.

We welcome strangers in the little ways we open ourselves up to them. Let's consider what it means to be the "other." The other is the one who is not like me. She is the liberal if I am conservative, and rich if I am poor. He is the guy who does not go to the same places I go, the family that does not worship where I worship or shop where I shop. The other is the person from the neighborhood I avoid; the guy I don't want sitting next to me on the plane.

When Father Dan needs rest and rejuvenation he sometimes takes a break at a small cottage on a lake in Ontario. Near the cottage is a little gas station where he buys a few groceries and picks up a daily newspaper. One day he noticed they also rented a few movies.

Recently, Dan went into the gas station for his loaf of bread and newspaper and noticed the videos were gone. When he asked the owner about it, making small talk, the man flew into a rage about the migrant workers. He called them all thieves, lumping them all under one label and demeaning the whole bunch. You have probably heard similar things.

What we notice most about the "other" is how much he or she is not like me. Most of us don't respond with the kind of vehemence Father Dan observed in the storeowner. Our negative opinion of strangers is usually a little quieter. We do not intentionally put people at a distance, but we can't help notice that there are some who are not like me.

Not like me—that's actually everyone, but some people seem particularly like a stranger because they are very different from the people I am comfortable with. We all tend to surround ourselves with people who agree with us on the vital issues, people who look like us, smell like us, have similar backgrounds, and hold similar convictions. It is natural to do this.

Our closest relationships are built on what we share and have in common. We build relationships at work, school, church, and in our neighborhoods. We meet people while we serve on the board of some local charity or in a service club. Thus we form a social sphere of people who are like us and do not feel like actual strangers. The problem with this manner of forming relationships is that we may exclude those who are not like us. We don't exclude them intentionally, but our worlds tend to be small and homogenous. We don't go looking to be made uncomfortable.

As a spiritual discipline, Benedict understood the importance of encountering those who are different from ourselves because it stretches us; it dislocates stiffness and opens us up to new possibilities. He meant for the monks to do so intentionally.

When we create a life surrounded by people just like ourselves, it is a very narrow life. We will not be challenged by such a life. We cave in on ourselves; our minds and spirits shrink to the pea-size of our world. A spirituality centered in such a life will drift into laziness and complacency. It is the kind of life that allows us to settle for easy answers based solely on personal experience. Letting ourselves believe that our experience constitutes normality and that other ways of doing life are abnormal is delusional and dangerous.

Lonni and her husband, David, are raising their granddaughter, Gina, who is now four years old. Recently, while Lonni was attending a dinner party, a woman asked her how the arrangement was working. Lonni replied that it worked fine and they enjoyed the child a lot.

"It must be very hard taking care of a young child at this point in your lives. You're to be admired for taking your family obligation so seriously when you could be enjoying your middle years instead. . . ."

Hard? Lonni thought, Taking care of Gina? No, it isn't hard. It is a gift to us. She stood toe-to-toe with the very gracious and kind woman, baffled that anyone would think such a thing would be considered an obligation or a difficulty. She thought of the other grandmothers she knew in similar situations and how most of them agreed with her: The opportunity to raise a grandchild, while complicated and often painful, is overwhelmingly a joy.

"We are grateful for Gina. She has never been a burden, and we count every day with her as a divine gift."

The woman who was talking tilted her head and gazed at Lonni as if she were an alien. How could that be? The question suspended in the air between the two women. It was as if they were speaking two different languages. The woman only knew what she would feel, and she assumed that it was the normal way to feel. She assumed it was how Lonni would feel, because Lonni seemed normal.

But Lonni didn't feel that way. Not a twinge or a molecule of such thoughts had ever passed through her. It was all simply gift: every breath the child takes, every running through the room and singing of childish songs, every good-night, every tear, and every giggle. It is all gift.

There was a deep difference between the two women. Lonni has buried three of her five daughters. You do not put tiny caskets into the ground without being changed. Lonni had realized young that every child is a gift. The sick child and the well child, the lovely child and the homely child. None could ever be a burden. God honors us with every gift of every child. This was Lonni's experience.

The other woman's experience was different. She had attempted to raise a son, teach school, and do the right thing by her son as a single mother. It had been a struggle, and she had denied herself many things. "Many things," the woman said, sighing deeply. "He will never know what I gave up for him." She loved her son but had not resolved the inner tension.

In telling Lonni her story the woman said, "It's hard not to resent what I gave up." Before hearing Lonni's story the woman had assumed that there is one way to react in such a situation, and that one way is the way *she* would feel.

Now the woman was not an awful person: she was a retired teacher, very involved with her community, a gracious woman. She had not considered before that her ideas were anything other than normal. But such assumptions keep our world small. It never even occurred to her that someone she considers "normal" of her own class, race, and religion would think or feel differently.

Lonni found the roles reversed a few days later when an old friend Clara, someone she had not heard from in several years, called. Clara's roommate of eleven years had died and Clara was planning to relocate to Arizona. Clara had lived in the top half of her house and her roommate Charles had lived in the lower half. Charles and Clara were long-time friends. Charles was an alcoholic, which Clara knew when she agreed to let him move in. For most of those eleven years, Charles had been a model roommate and a good friend. But in the last three years, the alcoholism had caused brain damage. Charles had needed someone to care for him. So Clara did. She hired help to assist her, but Clara still took most of the responsibility for feeding him and changing his bed and playing cards with him on his better days.

In response to Clara's news, Lonni replied, "I'm so sorry to hear you lost your friend. It must be a terrible loss. Is there anything I can do?"

Clara, always blunt, said, "Terrible loss? Oh honey, you don't understand, do you? I loved my friend, but his sickness kept me tied to him long after I would have asked him to leave if he had not been sick. Sure, I'll miss the Charles I knew once. I've missed him for a long time, even when Charles was alive. Now, I feel free for the first time in three years."

Hospitality means we don't tell people how to feel. We listen to them. We let them tell us how they feel. This is not easy for a compassionate person to do. We stir up the pot of our own emotion and experience, and the result is what *I* feel. How *I* would respond. How *I* would behave.

When someone dies, we naturally feel compassion for the loss. When we hear that someone's children have made choices that seem painful for the parents, we assume the parent is suffering. These are not negative assumptions. But, in relating to the person, we must offer them room to feel what they feel, rather than assuming that we know what they feel. Even if we think that we have been through exactly the same experience ourselves, we cannot know what another is feeling. Every person brings to an event their unique history and personality. You can assume that every parent who loses a child in an auto accident is grieving, but you can't know what that grief feels like for the parent. You only know if you offer an open space in yourself for them to pour out their feelings.

If we consider the possibility that others do not feel and think the same as we do, we suddenly feel very small in a mysterious, expansive universe. There is a security in a world where all the others are like me. It's a false security, but we prefer it to no security at all.

We admit it is hard to do otherwise. It is probably even a natural thing to establish self as the criteria for *normal*. The danger is that we will do so blindly and without any awareness of the pitfalls of our homogeneous world. The ramifications go beyond saying the wrong thing to the wrong person. When we hold tightly to a worldview in which our own experience is at the center, we live small lives. If we don't consider the ramifications of such a life we can easily slip into suspicion, misunderstanding, and prejudice of strangers—those who do not meet our standard of "normal."

Recently, a friend underwent surgery on her foot. As a result she could not bear weight on it for many weeks. After recovering from surgery enough to drive, she packed her wheelchair and crutches into her Jeep and headed up to the cabin in the woods for some rest. When she arrived at the cabin, alone, a young man was reading the electric meter.

She had planned, on arrival, to call the neighbor (who was expecting her call) for assistance in carrying everything into the house. Instead, the very nice young man helped carry everything into the house, parked her car in the garage, and offered to help unpack and take upstairs anything that needed to go there. When she called her husband to tell him she had arrived, she also mentioned the meter reader and how helpful and gracious he had been. Her husband replied, "Yeah, we'll see if he was really being nice, or will he back tonight after dark?" We have all conditioned ourselves toward suspicion.

Suspicion is one of the enemies of hospitality. Fear is at the core of suspicion. We are all starved for love, yet we are mostly unwilling to trust others to give us what we need. We grow callous and hesitant from the fear, always waiting for the other shoe to drop, ever sure of the next rejection. So, we keep people at a distance with suspicion and fear. We fear not only rejection and harm, we fear being used or trapped by love. We fear we will give too much of ourselves and receive nothing or little in return.

Another enemy of hospitality is narcissism. When we place the great "I" at the center of our universe, we give no value to anyone else. We make commodities of people, consuming them for our personal enrichment and happiness. It's common in our culture. The other's only purpose is what he or she can do for us. For many, the only thing that matters is what works for them. There is a kind of contempt in this utilitarian view of others.

You may remember the classic Disney movie *Peter's Dragon* starring Helen Reddy and Mickey Rooney. It is the story of an orphaned boy who has an invisible dragon as a companion. In one scene the townspeople, mostly fishermen, blame the boy because they aren't catching fish. One of them yells, "There's no room here for you."

"There's Room for Everyone" is the song that follows this comment. The lyrics counter the idea that some people don't belong.

> There's room for everyone in this world if everyone makes some room. Won't you move over and share this world, will everyone make some room. . . . give him a chance to sing his song, he only wants to belong. . . . a Dragon is just one more stranger in search of a friend. . . . step aside, let them live, it's simple to give, like us they just need a home. . . . Love given freely can spare this world. . . just give an inch, give a yard, never flinch when the time comes to give a hand. Let's all make sure we give everyone someplace to stand, just the way God planned.

Hospitality makes room even for the one who is frighteningly different—the dragon, you might say. Hospitality treats people respectfully, as if they are sacred, because they are. Even the other, the stranger, the one who is nothing at all like me. He brings the Divine to me, too.

We falsely comfort ourselves by assuming that others are like us. We think that all sensible people must think this, or think that. We Americans think that all good families must be upset when their adult children return home. We view this as some sort of failure on the part of the adult child, whereas there are many reasons adults might live with their parents and vice versa. In most countries it is considered a good and healthy thing. In America, our culture encourages us to raise our children with a launch-them-into-their-own-family-and-own-life mentality. Most people around the world do not look forward to becoming strangers with their children.

By opening ourselves up to new people, we gain new ideas. We discover the world is filled with people who are nothing like us—and it is a delightful thing. The stranger helps us locate our favorite lies. The stranger helps us see the absurd in our culture and ourselves. The stranger opens our eyes.

Rather than hospitality, however, our culture too often exudes contempt. Our music and movies and television are filled with contempt. Get a life. Been there, done that. Ask me if I care. What part of "no" don't you understand? These are superior little snipes designed to make one person feel gleefully superior.

One friend told a story of buying magazines at the airport. The girl behind the counter went on to the next customer without giving our friend a bag. Another girl came up from a different part of the store and stood at the counter. Our friend asked for a bag and the girl said, "It's not my shift yet." This is the opposite of hospitality. It is an everyday, happens-much-too-often example of contempt.

Not far from your memory, no doubt, is an image of someone who pulled on big spiked boots and stomped all over your bare soul. It was deliberate. It happens to everyone. That person intended to make you feel small. They refused to make room for you, refused to acknowledge your right to be here.

It happened to Lonni one morning in a grocery store.

I was attempting to move down an aisle so I could get something on my list. Standing in the middle of the aisle was a well-dressed woman with two small children, probably her grandchildren. She looked about seventy. She was selecting a product from the shelves near the bread I was after. The children went to move and let me through. She shot them a paralyzing look and said, "Stay put. I am not finished yet."

Lonni was sure she meant those words for her, not the children. It appeared that she perceived others as having no right to share her space. She would not move over and make room on the planet for another. What do you do when faced with such a situation?

Benedict would say that you give the woman the space she is demanding. You patiently put up with the crankiness of human nature. When she is finished and moves away, you pick up your bread, and you don't lose your peace of mind over it. It is a small way to be hospitable to even a difficult person.

It isn't easy to be open and hospitable when you feel threatened. At the root of many less-than-welcoming attitudes toward others is fear. If I am not at home in my own skin, enough to let someone share my space, how will I ever be able to look on the stranger with anything like kindness and welcome?

Fear devastates our ability to trust, love, and open up to others. Most of our fears are completely without reason, but not all of them. It *is* reasonable to fear the out-of-control truck barreling down on us. Events and people can actually threaten our lives, threaten what is most important to us. Yet, it is *not* reasonable to fear every stranger or every new idea.

It's not easy to have what we cherish threatened. In a monastery, the monks live in a certain way. The day unfurls with prayer setting the pace. A monk can count on certain things happening at certain times, and he is pretty sure what face he will see around the next corner.

At least that was so for as long as Brother Benedict could remember. Brother Ben is the oldest member of the St. Benedict monastic community. He has served the community as cook, and until recently he cared for the cows.

The youth retreat ministry did not involve Ben most of the time. Sometimes when he was up late with a cow who was about to deliver her baby he would run into Father Dan as he passed the retreat house on the way to the barn. That was about it, until the year the monks decided to expand the youth retreat house, making it more comfortable for the kids, while improving the usefulness of the building.

During the building process, Dan and Mary had to take the teens over to the monastery for group projects and meals. Brother Benedict suddenly had teenaged girls in his kitchen. Giggling little girls, tossing their pretty heads and poking into the pots bubbling on the stove. Girls who looked shyly at him as if he were an alien in his own home. This is the kind of thing that can disrupt monastic life.

Ben had a quick smile for the girls. He became quite skilled at teasing the girls and making them laugh. Their presence was profoundly uncomfortable for him, yet he was friendly without exception. These children had overtaken his beloved monastery and his territory—the kitchen—and yet he was called on, by all that is Benedictine, to see in them the presence of the Divine.

So that's what he did. He accepted his current lot in life and tried to enjoy the children who threatened life as he knew it. The girls just loved him. They were always telling Father Dan how much they loved the monk in the kitchen.

A few years later, when the monastery opened up Sunday mass to visitors, there was another period of adjustment, and it would have been natural for the monks to feel that their way of life was threatened again. Even if some of them were wrestling with the decision, they extended a warm welcome to the strangers invading their home and gathered them gently into the monastic family. It was not always easy for the monks, but they soon discovered how visitors and guests enriched the monastic life.

Dan recalls how risky it all felt at the time:

"Looking back over our history, I can see now how two decisions drastically changed our lives as monks: inviting high-schoolers onto our property for retreats beginning in 1975, and welcoming people to our Sunday and daily masses starting in the mid-1990s. In both cases, one would think the welcoming would have been automatic; we are, after all, monks. But it was not a given, because of our unique history."

The monks who founded St. Benedict in 1959 had the vision of the monastery as a novitiate, a place to grow new monks who would then live, love, and minister in the parishes in Detroit. The founding monks had lived monastic life the best they could in parish settings, but they were aware that bustling parishes were not conducive to the growth and development of young monks.

They were not prepared for the new batch of monks to fall in love with the monastic life, outside of a parish setting. Dan was one of those baby monks who first came to St. Benedict's under the fledgling program.

"I was one of a group of young monks who were not interested in serving the parish, except for perhaps a brief time. I wanted to be a monk, a make-a-place-in-the-quiet-and-find-God-in-the-woods kind of monk."

The Benedictine community, Father Dan admits, stuck with the novitiate perspective for too long. For fifteen years, almost no one other than monks set foot on the monastery grounds. "It was almost a siege mentality," Dan remembers, "Us against them, and if they approached we went into under-siege tactics. There was no malice involved, but it was wrong, and it was not Benedictine."

People would call and ask, "Do you have a mass on Sunday that is open to the public?" The young monks were trained to respond, "Well, yes we do, but our mass is very early and we're hard to find and we are not a parish. Have a blessed day." The not-too-veiled message was: stay away. St. Benedict would have throttled the monks.

The ice began to crack in 1975. God was moving in the community. From 1965 to 1969, Dan had been sent to the University of Toronto to study theology. It was there he first worked with youth. After ordination, the community sent him to serve in their big parish in Detroit.

"It was again against my wishes. Neither Toronto or Detroit was my idea of a monastic setting."

However, the young monk was growing in his vocation. Benedictine monks are taught to listen. Listen with the heart and not just the ear. What was expected to be one year at the Detroit parish turned into six. During those years, he again worked with youth, and he met the woman who would be his partner in youth retreat work.

"When I finally returned to St. Benedict Monastery in 1975, youth ministry and the normal work of lawn mowing, barn cleaning, and ditch digging were the only kinds of work I knew how to do. So, I proposed to my brother monks that we use a then-unoccupied former barn, that had been remodeled to house young monks and was presently a library, as a youth retreat house. Okay, the idea had its flaws. There was no dining room, kitchen, conference room, chapel, or much of anything you would need for youth retreats, not even adequate bathroom facilities."

The community was game. After some debate they responded with an overwhelming, "Yes! Let's try it."

To date about eighty thousand teenagers have made a retreat with the Benedictines on the hill in Oxford.

The building was remodeled several years later, then a couple other times, and eventually it tripled in size. They named it Subiaco after St. Benedict's cave. The young people even have used the name of the place to describe the experience itself: "This is my fourth Subiaco. . . ."

The 1975 opening of the monastery to teenagers has affected more lives than can possibly be numbered. When the teenagers walk into Subiaco and look around at the expansive, warm, and beautiful retreat house, they often respond with, "Wow, I can't believe that this is all for us!" You should see their faces when it dawns on them that monks are scrubbing their toilets and showers.

But, the 1975 opening of the monastery to youth did something for the monks too. Mary Cummings, who helped with the teen retreats from the beginning, became a friend of the community. Even crusty old Brother Ben embraced her, because he could see the good she was doing for the monks and the retreat youth. She was the first nonmonastic to become involved in the life of the community on a regular basis. She opened the way for the many who would become friends of the community. The next opening up happened about ten years ago, when the monks moved Sunday mass to a reasonable hour of the morning and opened it to the public.

"When we looked back on all those phone calls and the people we discouraged from coming to mass, we wondered if perhaps those calls were inspired by God to get our attention," says Father Dan.

As you would expect in most monasteries, the majority of monks are introverted by nature. This opening up to outsiders was an enormous mountain they had to climb. Despite the peril, the monks could see something holy was happening among them, and they were determined to increasingly welcome the visitor. Almost all monasteries (including Trappists) are open to the public to some degree, at least on Sundays, but this has been new to the monks of St. Benedict Monastery.

They opened the doors and the people came: neighbors, friends, former retreatants and their families, people they had met in parish work, and many, many strangers. All have told the monks, over and over, how grateful they are for the opportunity to celebrate mass with them and share in their life in some small way.

"But we monks know the truth about all this; we are the ones who have received the most from the whole deal," says Father Dan. "We monks were endangered by our isolation. Our identity as Benedictines was threatened because we were disconnected, oblivious to the world beyond our gate. We were professional prayers watching from our view on the hill.

"We have discovered that we are grounded in real life in a way that can happen only by encountering real people. It is easy to pray for 'the world' and 'God's people' when you don't have to look into their tear-reddened eyes, or fetch more toilet paper after mass on Sunday. Something sacred and unexpected has happened since we opened our doors and our hearts. Without blurring the line between our monastic family and their families, we have become part of each other's lives."

It is always easier to care for the world, to care for all the others, from a distance. We can even feel good about our prayers for them as long as the people are not in our space and are not taking up emotional space in our hearts. They become harder to handle when they show up and expect something from us.

The hardest thing about all these people is their absolute otherliness, which cannot be tamed or ignored. They are going to remain unlike us. We are not going to understand them.

We should celebrate this. We need them to be different from us. It fits in the way the universe has been designed.

We don't have to make a choice about how we will respond to others, as long as they stay on their side of the fence. In the wilderness of relationships, we contend with powers we'd rather not ever meet up with. We will keep opening the door, and keep making an attempt, and then one night will find us in some holy place and in a holy moment that snatches the breath away.

You will be tucking a child into bed, or pouring a second cup of coffee for your neighbor, or sharing a breadstick with your friend. You will be trying to know what is holy in us all and wondering how to be known by the Holy. You will have read a few books and maybe taken a workshop. You will have spent some time with people reputed to be experts on the subject of hospitality. You will wing it more often than not.

And then that splinter of light will get through the great mysterious confusion, who knows when or where or why, and grace will sneak up on you and you will know, if only for a splintered flash of a second, you will know that your trying is making a difference and your trying is enough.

On a day like that, all the others you have been trying to let into your weary heart will seem at home in your heart, and like the monks Father Dan tells us about, you will know that you and all the others are really part of each other.

four

Cloister, Community, and Hospitality

Cloister, community, and hospitality: these three together make up a healthy relational ability. They are all tangled together and impossible to separate completely. Hospitality starts at home, after all. And you do not become good at loving the strain of being together in a family or a community if you have not yet learned to be alone.

For our purpose let us clarify, exactly, what we mean by each term. We are not saying these are the only definitions that can be used for these words. we're just telling you how we are going to use the words in this chapter.

Cloister refers to the time a monk is alone, or you are alone. It is the apartness of solitude and silence. We use *community* to refer to your closest relationships, the people with whom you share your life. The monk shares life with his community of brother monks. *Hospitality* refers to your interactions in all other relationships, especially those outside the security of your comfort zone—relationships with the stranger.

One of the most fascinating things about a monastery is how the monks manage to keep all the facets of their life together in balance. This ability is especially remarkable when some of those facets would appear to be opposites, such as solitude and community.

At the monastery there is always time for prayer, always time to linger with a friend, always time for a needed nap. Work is accomplished as it should be, but in a healthy monastic setting the monks don't obsess over it. The monk has time alone and also time to gather with his community for meals and recreation and meetings.

The triad *cloister*, *community*, and *hospitality* represent this balance. These three threads of monastic life weave together to make a strong whole: a whole life and a whole person. Many of us feel we are lacking balance in our lives. We wonder why it is that when life splinters into a million directions we also feel splintered.

In considering the deeper meanings of *cloister*, *community*, and *hospitality*, we can begin to discern how and where our lives are out of kilter. Are we spending too much time with others and not enough time alone? Are we constantly in social settings and ignoring the most important relationships? Have we isolated ourselves altogether from relationships?

Relationships between monks living in a monastery operate by the same dynamics as your relationships. The monks are a group of men who are committed to going to God together. It is their life together that most profoundly shapes who they become as human beings. Within the monastery, cloister, community, and hospitality represent three states of relating.

Each of these is dependent on the other. They are woven together to create the whole of monastic life. Life outside the monastery is very similar. We need time alone (cloister), we need time with those closest to us (community), and we need to open ourselves to those who are not one of us (hospitality).

The monastic day is purposeful about keeping its holistic balance. The community has time together at prayer, during meals, and in working together and recreation. Silence is a normal part of every monastic day, usually during meals and at other times of the day, such as the silence that begins after night prayer and ends after breakfast or Morning Prayer. Benedict knew the monastery would never be without guests, so he told monks to weave them into their monastic day with reverence and welcome.

Some people, especially those with young children, find it difficult to structure their lives according to this pattern. The trick is to think of it as a pattern and not a model to follow after slavishly. The monastic model simply reminds us to take time for what matters most. Balance your relationships. Take time for those closest to you, be more open to strangers, and do not forget to take time to be alone. We all need regular doses of solitude and silence.

Most of us cannot long escape our relationships. People who want our attention surround us. The hardest thing can be carving out time for silence. Our contemporary lives are hectic and noisy. We are driven by devices, surrounded by machines. We have grown comfortable with the background noise. How often have you turned on the radio or television just to have the noise, without even thinking about it? Every day you see people driving a car, jogging, reading a newspaper with noise attached to their ears. This does more than keep people at a distance; it keeps life at a distance and also keeps us from noticing what is going on inside us.

Silence is related to solitude. In the monastery there are long periods of silence: meals taken in silence, silent prayer, and hours of solitude. Silence and solitude are related, and we are terrified of them both.

When we are alone, we have cut off our normal routes to self-escape. Not only that, solitude hacks off most of the usual ways we feel affirmed. In solitude we cease being competent workers. We do not serve and nurture others in solitude, and we seldom talk. Once amputated from these normal support systems, we discover a throbbing restlessness begins to surface.

Thomas Keating, monk and author, calls this the "unloading of the unconscious." What's happening? Ancient wounds to the psyche begin ascending into the conscious region of the mind, they float up like long-dead bodies. Illusions shatter around us and wisdom gets a chance to get hold of us. If we stick with the process we will know the truth about ourselves. All the glorious truth.

But the bountiful good of the truth does not come until we've danced with a few demons long hidden in the psyche. This is when most people turn on the radio, get in the car, or hustle home to the safety of people, noise, and activity. The purpose of spirituality is not to keep this moment from happening; rather, spirituality will eventually bring it on.

Some people find that in their first experiences of solitude and silence they wrestle with frightful emotions and fantasies. Some dark void in them beckons them to jump over the edge. It does not take long to realize why we avoid ourselves.

If you stay with solitude, you discover that this inner void is your friend. It is your true hunger. It has God's name on it. It tells you the truth about yourself, once you are able to push aside all the garbage that initially erupts out of it.

The first stirrings of loneliness, when you are alone, emerge from a vast inner emptiness that can rattle us beyond what we expected. It is then you'll understand what it means to refer to solitude as a state of the mind, rather than a place and time.

We possess inward solitude at a very high cost. It does not come easily. In solitude, we feel helpless and almost out of control. We have grown dependent on others and the noises we make at each other. We do not even know how to imagine our lives without the entire bustle.

A friend of Lonni's asked her what she does when she goes off alone. She wanted to know what a typical day was like. Lonni told her that she rests and prays. She writes a little, she takes a walk or does some work around the cabin, then she might pray again and maybe read or listen to music. Her friend smiled and replied, "Well, okay, that's a morning. What do you do the rest of the time?"

Once, while making a retreat at the monastery, Lonni was staying in the retreat house and had a window cracked a bit. She overhead two monastic novices wondering out loud what she could be doing in there alone all this time. They were inexperienced in the monastic life and had not yet learned that one does not need to be a monk to practice silence and solitude.

One man who takes regular solitary retreats took his cell phone with him last year. He says his seventeen-year-old son called three times a day the first two days. Finally the boy asked, "Are you okay, Dad? Is there something we need to talk about?" Solitude is frightening for some and simply baffling for others.

The cloister, or solitude, is as much a state of mind as it is a place. This state of mind develops through the practice of solitude. With an inner solitude in place, you do not mind being alone, because you know you are never alone. You do not resist and fear others, because you know they are not a threat, they can't control you. They do not determine your worth as a human being. You have nothing you must prove to them.

Solitude, rather than driving us into ourselves and away from others, propels us outward and opens us up. It is from the hours spent alone that a monk comes to cherish relationships. It is from the silence that he learns to listen. It is in the deep, empty place inside himself that the monk finds God.

No one can practice genuine Benedictine hospitality unless they have come to it through solitude. We can go through the motions, but the inner opening up does not happen until we have spent a good deal of time alone and a genuine self-love is born. Solitude is built into the monastic life. If you are not a monk, you will have to find ways to build it into yours.

Look for solitude in the snatches of time that hurry past unnoticed. While you wait for a friend to arrive, while the kids are playing, while your spouse watches television, before the household is awake, or after everyone is in bed. Find a quiet place to sit still. Shut the door. Turn off the lights if this will help and light a candle.

One woman has a place of solitude on a rickety sunporch attached to the back of her house. It is separated from the house by glass sliding doors. On that porch are a big chair, bookshelves, a crucifix, and a few personal items. If the sliders are pulled and the drapes closed, her family knows it means, "Don't bother me now, please. I need to be alone." On the other hand, when the door is open, others are welcome to join her in that special place.

Somehow, her family understands that they have to mean business if they join her. This is not the place for discussing the weather or the grocery list. That sunporch has become a place where her teenagers talk about their dark secrets and wild dreams, and her husband talked his way through a vocational crisis. Solitude creates a place that is wide enough to make room for others. Teen retreats at the monastery are a weekend long. At one point in the weekend, the teens are instructed to find a quiet place, alone, and they are given a reflective exercise to complete. It is not a very long exercise and the child is really not alone; lots of other people are in the building. Yet the young people report that they have never had an experience of solitude before. The usual thing they do if they find themselves alone (and adults as well) is to seek company in music or television. The noise companions them, and then they are never really alone with the big *alone* that lives in all of us. New monks often struggle with the periods of silence and solitude in the monastery.

The important thing we learn from these three threads of monasticism is that we must find a way to weave together all the fragments, splinters, and scatterings. Contradictions will always pull at us. We will want time to ourselves while acknowledging the rights others have to our time and energy.

Working through the seeming contradictions that pull us in various directions is always complex. Rather than looking for easy answers, we can model our relationships after the monks and embrace a wide spectrum of relationships, from acceptance of the self to acceptance of the stranger.

The longer we wander through this world the more sure we become that our companions are of utmost importance, as important as our solitude. We don't need to pick solitude over family, or family over other relationships. We need to attentively set our hearts on balancing it all.

Companions give us the support we need to go on. They provide the tenderness of friendship and are a source of stability, wisdom, and growth. We need other people. Some of our companions we choose, such as friends or a spouse. But we are born with a whole set of relationships, for better or worse.

We all are given a family as part of the cost of our humanity. If, by some set of circumstances, we do not have a family we tend to create one for ourselves. Do we believe these relationships are pure chance? The monks can help us understand that what seems to be chance is God waiting to be discovered. The monk is taught to look for God's presence in every other monk he lives with. He does this with the guys he doesn't particularly like, maybe even more so with the ones he does. He believes that it is no accident that they are together in the monastery.

Our families seem to be rather happenstance. We don't get to pick them, and they almost always come with a lot of weirdness that leaves us toting around a heavy weight for most of our lives. There are few challenges greater than the attempt to be hospitable to those closest to us. Some of it is that they are so close. Some of it is that we assume they will love us, regardless of how we treat them. Some of it, maybe, is just bad habit.

If you asked Father Michael Green, one of the monks of St. Benedict Monastery, for an image of what a monastery is about, he would most likely tell you that it is a family. This is an interesting analogy because the monks are a rare sort of family. They did not grow up together. They don't share a history of celebrations, tragedies, and tradition. The members of the family don't all have the same odd-shaped front teeth and they don't share a last name. They are strangers. They are brothers.

This is very different, in one sense, from our biological families. We do have shared histories, shared jokes, and family legends. We all remember Dad's funeral and we remember the day someone walked out the door and never came back. We are haunted by what someone said twenty-five years ago. But, we are also strangers. It didn't happen overnight. One day you woke up forty years old and realized your sibling is no better known to you than the person next door.

The woman who was mother to a five-year-old is not the same woman who is your mother when you are forty-five. Mothers and fathers give themselves over to caring for their young, they protect and train and shelter. They almost cease to be an individual "me" while they are raising children, and so it is not odd that a child hardly ever knows what their parents' dreams are and have been. They do not know the parent as a real person. They do not know what their father gave up to be their father, and they don't know what their mother's beautiful, deep dream is about.

The day you hear that your father danced on roller skates, and your mother sang in nightclubs, you experience disorientation, as if it has to be someone else's father or mother being described. Most often we have lines in our skin long before we ever begin to trace the lines of our beloved parent's face, looking for the mystery of who lurks there behind those familiar eyes. About the time we are mature enough to realize our parent is a stranger, through no fault of their own, they are taken from us.

We need hospitality in these closest of relationships. Every now and then you get so tired that you just want to be with people who don't require an explanation.

Family can be that. People who know why you're tired, and have been wishing for a long while that you would put up your feet and shut your eyes.

Even if you do not spend a lot of time with your brothers and sisters, you know, on a gut level, that they understand how you are made, they know from whence you came. You have lived your lives side by side for a lifetime. No, they have not been part of your everyday life, but neither are they oblivious to you. They know where it hurts. They know the long strings of mistakes and second chances you've accumulated. They know the bits and pieces of what, all strung together, makes you who you are today.

The other day Lonni had a spat with her sister Lorri. They are the only girls in a family of seven siblings. When Lonni was a little girl with four brothers, she prayed for a sister, and she got one. But they don't often agree. Every now and then they discover some odd thing they share, which they don't share with anyone else in the family, or in the world for that matter. For example, they both sleep hugging a pillow, and if you ask either of them what their favorite movie of all time is they will reply "*The King and I.*" They are both big Don Henley fans. What are the chances unless you are sisters?

But on this particular day the two sisters were fighting. They misunderstood each other and pushed each other's buttons. After some pretty intense e-mail bickering, the true Benedictine spirit rose up in Lonni, and she told her sister to go to hell. To which Lorri replied, "You don't have to care what I think and you probably don't. But I'm not one of your friends you can dismiss, and I'm not going away just because you want me to. I am your sister." It's hard to get rid of a sister, or a brother, even if you try. And, if by some awful circumstance you do get rid of one for good, it will break you heart forever.

That is what your sister (or brother) gives you—a stubborn, everlasting kind of relationship that will make you weep and make you lose your temper. She knows where you came from. Deny it, suppress it, paint it a different color, and there she is holding on to the truth you would rather not look at today, thank you.

Now all of that is very good for us on one hand. We need to stand in the middle of our messiness and know we are loved and accepted. When a family can offer such acceptance, it is a glorious and holy thing. However, we hit a serious snag in our family relationships when we refuse to let family members grow up, change, and become people who are different from our ideas about them. Yes, we share a history with our family, but there are large sections of history we do not share. Some regions of ourselves are completely unknown to our families.

In many ways we are exactly like those monks who are strangers and yet family. We are not united by a vow to share life together, but in our families we end up sharing life anyway. We stick in our families because we believe family is important. We do what we consider the right thing, and that's a lot like a vow, so you keep to it in the good and the bad.

You don't walk away because your sister and your wife have words. You don't break your mother's heart because she doesn't meet your enlightened adult standard of motherhood. None of us ever keep our vows perfectly, but vows are still worth making and working very hard to keep—especially when it isn't easy.

By being hospitable with one another, monks give each other permission to be odd or cranky, or just a little off sometimes. There is room in this "family" for those on the edge and those who put you on edge.

There is room for the quiet and boisterous, room for the weak and the strong in this family.

Benedict tells his monks to "anticipate one another in honor; most patiently endure one another's infirmities, whether of body or of character" (*The Rule of St. Benedict* 72). God, after all, receives both the glory and the wreck we make of our lives. We owe it to one another to do no less, even in our families. Family is a good place to start practicing hospitality.

We look for ways to weave together the fragments of our lives. We want to feel whole and we want to see how one thing relates to another. Constant change makes us fearful, even insecure. We cannot expect our closest relationships to give us what we can receive only in solitude. We cannot expect solitude to give us what only intimate relationships are capable of giving us, and we must not expect that every relationship can bear the full weight of intimacy.

We started out talking about the three strands of monasticism: cloister, community, and hospitality. Each is important. You must spend time alone. It need not be long blocks of time, and you do not have to go far away, but you need a door you can close as well as a place inside of you where you can be in solitude.

We also need others, including people who are not close to our heart of hearts. We need simpler, uncomplicated relationships with others. Hospitality expects that we share ourselves, some part of ourselves at least— some sliver of time, some mere insight, or just a slice of peanut butter pie with someone who needs a slice of peanut butter pie and a smile. "Benedictine spirituality is intent on the distribution of self for the sake of the other," writes Benedictine author Joan Chittister in *Wisdom Distilled from the Daily*.

In the fall of 1999 a rather odd man appeared in Hazelton, Pennsylvania. He wore a white robe and no shoes. He had long hair and a beard. Residents claim the gloom in that coalmine-wrecked town lifted the day he walked in, and local religious leaders say people showed up in the pews who had abandoned the halls of faith long ago.

Carl Joseph, who calls himself "What's-Your-Name," looks like a storybook picture of Jesus right down to the twinkle in his eye. Carl Joseph is about forty years old, and in the last decade he has wandered through thirteen countries and forty-seven states. He is reportedly in Virginia at this writing.

While in Pennsylvania, Mr. Joseph received a lot of

press, something he did not go looking for; he is much harder to locate now that he is avoiding press coverage. Every now and then a story will surface from a town he has visited. He owns only what he wears, and he lives with whoever opens a door to him. He has been arrested in Ohio twice, for refusing to break up a crowd of teenagers gathered around him.

He does not claim and has never claimed to be Jesus. Someone, though, attacked him once for impersonating Christ. Apparently that person had not read what the Gospels say about becoming more like Jesus.

Carl Joseph is a traditional Catholic who wants people to respect the Church and believe in Jesus. As many as two thousand people have shown up at one of his town meetings where he talks about love and grace. Then he moves on to the next town, and in his wake, people report that their lives are changed.

It's not hard to figure out that people respond to him the way they do because he is a living icon. They know he isn't Jesus, well of course they know. They aren't stupid folks in Ohio or Pennsylvania. But we *want* Jesus to be among us. We want him to listen, we want him to touch us, we want to hear him laugh and tell us a story. If Carl Joseph is willing to be an icon, a lot of people are willing to let him.

We heard about a child who was feeling ill. His mother was at work and he was home with a babysitter. The mother called home to tell the sick boy that she loved him and that she is always with him, even when they are apart. The child responded, "But, Mommy, I want someone in skin." That's what we need, you and me and all those messy others. We just want someone in skin.

Not very long ago Father Dan's mother become very ill and had to be moved into a nursing facility. It was a bright, clean place with caring, well-trained people. The kind of place where you believe your mother will be safe and cared for carefully. But his mother described the facility best when she said to him, "They kiss you good-night here." It is human touch that makes us feel most human.

We become more available as the one "in skin" for others as we move toward a healthy balance in our relationships. Balance gives us freedom, it eases anxieties, and it makes room in our lives. Cloister, community, and hospitality—they represent this balance. Enter each deeply. Know the depths of solitude, enjoy the warmth of community, and take a hand in the companionship of hospitality. By gently and gradually gathering up the strands of your fragmented life into one whole, you will become the one in skin that can distribute yourself to others, and still have something left to take into the great solitude of your vast soul and rest in God.

five

Preparing a Table

Uncle Stan dies in Cleveland and you find yourself sitting at a table with cousins you haven't seen in years and great-uncles you did not even remember. The death is a sad thing, but there at the tables during lunch you hear stories about your dad. You hear how your parents met. Someone remembers the time you visited cousin Linda and cried to go home to your mother, but Linda is gracious enough not to mention you were a big, strong boy of eleven at the time.

The table is a place where you connect and belong. It is a place where the past remains alive in the memory of the very old, and the future sparkles with possibility. It is enchanted. We lean close together, we share a glass, we tell a story. Through this simple human relating, the universe feels as though it is right again, even after Uncle Stan has gone on to whatever comes next.

We all have memories of tables prepared for us and those we have readied for others. Some of the memories are from childhood. Others are memories of good friends, of falling in love, or of deeply connecting with another human being. Meals are powerful symbols in our memory. But someone has to make a meal happen. Someone must consider it important enough to give themselves to the work that goes into preparation.

Setting a table and making ready for a meal involves preliminary thought and consideration for others. To do it right you have to think through your guest's preferences and history; you need to know if they have allergies or chronic illnesses. If you invite more than one guest, you must consider which of them would enjoy sitting together and how they might relate. Preparing for another pulls us out of ourselves—that is one of the good gifts of hospitality.

The image of preparing a table, or preparing a place, is a good overall image for hospitality. In genuine hospitality we work to make our entire existence a welcoming table, a place prepared for others to be at ease, to receive from us comfort and strength.

Hospitality teaches me to work at becoming someone who is easy to be with, as either guest or host.

Hospitality becomes a way of life as we become more open. It will not happen without preparation and unless you intend it to happen. When we speak of "preparing a table," we refer to the intention and the work of making space for another human being.

Preparing a table has sacramental meaning for Benedictines. Every meal, like every encounter with a human being, has the potential to reveal God present in Creation. The table represents the unknown yearning of every human heart for communion with the "something more" that infuses all that exists.

A lifetime of ignoring the sounds of the soul have deafened us to this universal desire, but some little part of us can't forget and waits eagerly for the moment bread is broken, a hand is given, a laugh fills the air, and then by chance or grace, a connection to someone happens that magically opens us up in places we didn't know existed.

Food is basic to human existence, but it is more than it seems to be; it represents the More. In the Christian tradition, bread and wine are sacramental. In every family meal, in every dinner between friends, in every meal where monks go to the table, a sacramental mystery is present. There is magic in these connections that does something to us way down deep. The lesson is that we must take seriously our receiving of others. Whether we are cooking a meal, mowing the grass, scouring the sinks, or painting a wall, we are preparing for the Sacred to come to us.

The monastery feeds dozens of teenagers almost every weekend during the school year. Brother Antony is the one who sets the tables. Besides being a monk, Antony is an artist. If you watch him setting tables in the retreat house you will probably guess he is an artist, even if you have never seen his studio. He prepares the tables for the teens with a sense of reverence that is obvious and humbling. He is setting places for pizza and soda, but he does so with the same care he uses when he prepares the table for Eucharist.

Antony understands that in preparing a table, he is not just setting a place to eat. He is making room for one of God's children. He is creating a space for a human being, and human beings are sacred. This means you do it right, you pay attention, you get out of yourself and whatever else might be occupying your mind.

The quieter teens especially respond to Antony, maybe because he's quiet himself. He moves behind the scenes of the retreat, preparing and putting people at ease, weaving his wondrous magic of beauty in everything he touches.

Many young adults who go to the monastery will remember their weekend for all their life. Many of them return to the monks to baptize their children and solemnize their marriages. They visit for Easter and Christmas. They show up when the bottom has fallen out of their lives. Somehow, a whole lot of them understand that the monks care about them.

Father Dan says that is because the monks take care in the little things. Like Brother Antony setting the table as if he were creating a work of art. Antony is Benedictine and he has heard over and over that the tools of the monastery are sacred. He understands that places and things mediate God. There was one incident, Dan remembers, when he really got to see the heart of Brother Antony.

"Because his understanding of Benedictine reverence for all things goes so deep, I should not have been surprised when his protective urges took over on one retreat. It is usual for the retreat team to tell the teens that when the pizza arrives they have to eat in an orderly fashion, not taking more than they can eat, and waiting for grace to be said.

"For some reason the pizza arrived one Sunday without one of us having issued the standard warning, and the kids converged on the pizza man with all the hormonal energy you can imagine in a fifteen-year-old.

"I was in the lower living room when Brother Antony came running down the steps and halted halfway, his face flushed. He said in his regal way, 'Father Dan, come at once. There's a chaos up here!' Then he turned on his heel and ran back to defend the retreat house with his last breath. You have to admire a guy who takes on forty-five hungry kids for the sake of what he considers holy."

The deep meaning of hospitality involves our entrance into the mess of things; it means we run right into the chaos if that's what it takes. If we do this, there is a slow, mysterious something that happens, transforming the riot into something good. Naturally, the hard thing is stopping ourselves from making for the door when the chaos happens. The hard thing is throwing yourself headlong into the riot and trusting the reality of transformation. We aren't going to run toward the riot unless we think transformation is worthwhile.

The retreat house at St. Benedict's was designed with teenagers in mind. The monks, architect, and workers kept this goal carefully in sight. It was built to be a shelter for teens, and it was meant to be the kind of shelter they would remember all their lives.

That is the kind of shelter hospitality offers: the staying kind. The purposes of hospitality are not as simple as providing comfort for a night or a week. The best kind of hospitality seeps into your soul and shapes your identity. We can give this kind of hospitality to each other only if we take the time to prepare sheltering places around us and inside of us.

The table set for the teens is one example of hospitality. But you set other kinds of tables all your life. We all eat and drink with others; rarely would we elect to dine alone. When you ask someone to your table, as these teens are invited to the monks' table at the retreat house, you include them, you make them part of "us." There are times when the food we share is a sign of connection and acceptance, times such as weddings, funerals, anniversaries, birthdays, graduations, family reunions, and religious professions. At these events food is a sign of unity and singleness of purpose.

In Latin, the word *companion* literally means to "break bread" together. No wonder the Eucharist has such power. It is founded in our food experience, and our earliest experience of that is associated with warmth and touching. Food is powerful. It says, "You belong here." It comforts.

It isn't just food we pass out that nourishes or impoverishes the human heart. The table, for the teacher or social worker, is her or his desk. Whatever the specific physical structures of your work might be, you give something to others from them. You create a space for others because work is always for the service of others.

In the ancient world (the one Jesus was born into), people saw the sharing of meals as having eternal consequences. If you ate meals with the right kind of people, paradise waited for you. If you ate with the wrong kind of people . . . well, you get it. Jesus challenged this organizing principle of his culture. Understanding how the culture viewed having the "right" dinner companions shines a whole new light on the old story of feeding the five thousand. People marvel at a little bit of food feeding a whole bunch of people and miss a whole other point. Jesus wanted them to *EAT* together. If they did this, it would change everything, they would be joining the revolution.

There's something to think about the next time we're washing windows or trimming the hedge. When we take an open stance toward others in all that we do, the work of our hands takes on transforming power. And that is a little thing we can do every day of our lives. We can pay attention to how we wax the floor and park the car because we are growing in awareness that the work we do is work for others.

Our preparations for others remind us that we are not alone in the world. Not only are we not alone, others are counting on us. Many years ago the monastery had a novice, an older novice who had the responsibility of ringing the bell that called the monks to prayer. He fell asleep early one night and woke up suddenly, thinking it was early. It was actually 10:30 P.M. He looked at his watch upside-down and thought he was twenty minutes late ringing the bell.

He rushed outside to the courtyard in his underwear, with his pants wrapped around his neck, and started ringing the bell as if everything in the world depended on what he was doing. Another monk, visiting from a sister monastery in Australia, stuck his head out the window and yelled in his Aussie way, "You bloomin' ass, it's only half past ten!" Nope, not even your best efforts will always be understood and appreciated.

Despite this, the novice recognized that his work was a service to others, a service he took seriously enough to run into the cold night in his underwear. (He told the other monks later that he wrapped the pants around his neck so he wouldn't catch cold.)

You can prepare for others every day in countless ways, and not just in the work you do from 9 to 5. You prepare for others when you plan a quiet time with your child, when you set candles on the dinner table, when you shovel your sidewalk, or trim the tree away from the street sign. These are ways of preparing to receive others—in other words, through these activities you prepare a table for others. When we are preparing a table, we are also preparing ourselves.

Our ability to make room for others, and the joy we do or do not find in such activity, depends largely on our experience of being accepted or not. We build shelter for others because somewhere along the way someone sheltered us and thereby taught our hungry heart how to love. Every little lesson along the way has accumulated to account for how we are able to love today.

Your memories of sheltering places may take you to a retreat house like Subiaco, or perhaps to your childhood. Every childhood has a sheltering place. Even children who are neglected or abused find sheltering places. Most of us don't have childhoods with such an extreme need for shelter. Instead, we have memories of rain falling on the roof of the porch, and we remember how safe and dry it felt there. Or, we remember the day the wind straight-lined across the woods and the only cover we could find was under the stairs, where Mom read a book and we sang while the wind roared. Those are the kinds of shelters that hold you during difficult times, long after the storm has passed. These are the sorts of shelters that families hope they can be for their children.

"Each summer day Gina and I nap under the whirling fan of the vaulted ceiling in the master bedroom," Lonni says. "She smells of chlorine from her little pool where she spent the morning under the trees that surround our cabin in the woods. She smells of peanut butter, and the sugary soda clinging to fingers that are wrapped tightly around her once-pink, but now very faded bunny. She keeps a thumb in her mouth. Her light brown hair is sun-streaked, and her long limbs are honey tan from the sunshine. We nap from 1:00 to 2:30 each day on the big bed, and before I fall asleep I remembering sleeping on a sunporch under the eaves of a house long ago. It was summer then, too, and raining.

"I don't know if this is actually a memory or a dream I recall. But I felt utterly safe in that place. There are spaces God creates like the wonderful oak-and-pine woods around our cabin, and there are spaces we make: our homes, offices, and the places we go to for the specific purpose of hearing God.

"Where Gina sleeps at the cabin is under the sharp slope of the cabin roof. It is a space otherwise useless. She sleeps there on two feather beds, three old quilts, and a sun-dried yellow-checkered sheet. Her little pillow has blue-and-white ticking; she refuses to use a pillowcase. There is a shelf that runs the length of her space. It's filled with odds and ends, much of it meaning nothing to anyone but Gina and me. Driftwood and shells from a walk on the beach, rocks collected from the bridge, a doll my daughter, her mother, loved as a little girl, a Madonna figure given to her by our very kind neighbor Florence. A dream-catcher hangs over her head. We got it at the dime store the morning after she had a bad dream. We agreed it wouldn't let any more bad dreams through."

Lonni says she has learned from the monastery that physical structures are more than brick, glass, and wood. Not that a building or home needs to be lavish to create a sense of security and shelter. Instead, we need to take care to create spaces where the soul can unfurl its wings and the toddler can wiggle her toes. This kind of care is in the details; it is revealed in our passion to prepare a place for someone. When we really care about someone, we try a bit harder.

Often, we don't give much thought to the kinds of places we are creating as we shape our homes. But what we make is holy. The work of human hands—monasticism has always considered that a sacred thing. We don't always notice it, sometimes this elusive reality strikes us at the oddest times. Author Frederick Buechner writes about such a time in *The Longing for Home: Recollections and Reflections*:

> Several winters ago my wife and I and our then twenty-year-old daughter, Sharmy, went to that great

tourist extravaganza near Orlando, Florida, called Sea World. There is a lot of hoopla to it—crowds of people, loud music, Mickey Mouse T-shirts, and so on, but the main attraction makes it all worthwhile. . . . The bleachers where we sat were packed.

The way the show began was that at a given signal they released into the tank five or six killer whales, as we call them . . . and no creatures under heaven could have looked less killerlike as they went racing around and around in circles. What with the dazzle of the sky and the sun, the beautiful young people on the platform and the soft southern air . . . it was as if the whole creation—men and women and beasts and sun and water and earth and sky and, for all I know, God himself—was caught up in one great, jubilant dance of unimaginable beauty. And then, right in the midst of it, I was astonished to find that my own eyes were filled with tears.

When the show was over and I turned to my wife and daughter beside me to tell them what had happened . . . there had been tears in their eyes also.

At St. Benedict Monastery the monks have built a chapel that, regardless of how often you go there, has the power to steal your breath and startle your eyes and move your soul. The chapel appears to have been raised up from the dust of the earth in a primal whirl of wind. It is a lot of glass and wood and modern architecture at its best, an architectural wonder actually. But it is much more than the plans that laid it out.

What the chapel has in common with Sea World is that it is the work of human hands; it was conceived in a human mind and crafted by human beings who were preparing a place for other human beings. This was always the intention.

Father Dan often spoke of the intention during the building process. "It will be a place you can go when you need to get away," he said. "It will be a refuge. A place of prayer where a little bit of peace can get inside of you." The chapel is the place where the monks go to pray day after day. It is also the place where they share their prayer and their life with the stranger at the door.

In human labor an astonishing thing happens: God shows up. As we prepare a place for others, something happens inside of us: We are prepared also. The Benedictine motto is "Pray and work." Benedictines consider work holy. Human labor is a reflection of divine work. Human labor is shared with God. Work expresses our humanity, and it gives us a chance to use our gifts. This mystical element to work expresses a sacramental understanding of life. Work requires reverence and it teaches us of our value. Former Eagles drummer Don Henley was very Benedictine when he wrote these lines in one of his songs, ". . . whatever your hands find to do, you must do with all your heart."

Through the many months the monks spent building their gloriously simple chapel, the community was preparing itself. They were making a conscious choice to include nonmonastics as part of their daily lives. The chapel allowed easier access to the monks. Before they had the new chapel, a visitor had to walk through the monastery to reach the chapel. People tended to be a little cautious about doing that, but the new chapel meant that people could join them for prayer or mass anytime. They could go and sit in the silence. People would be coming and going more than ever before.

The internal community preparations were subtle. Even the most introverted of monks began spending a few minutes with people after mass on Sunday. While the chapel was being raised up, relationships also were built. The monks were being true to their vision of opening up to God's people and welcoming them to share the journey.

At the same time, the monks had to prepare to guard their way of life, to set up boundaries that would protect the monastic community. Benedict made it clear to his monks that yes, they must open to strangers and welcome the stranger as if God were walking through the door. Benedict also told his monks, however, that after a greeting and a prayer they should excuse themselves from the guest. The monk had to learn to honor boundaries for himself and for the guest.

As they prepared for a new phase in their monastic life, the monks consciously made choices that would be welcoming. They paid attention to the details, such as providing a nursery for young children, determining how many people could be comfortable in the space, considering where the sun might hit the eyes of the people in the choir stalls and chairs. They worked on making sure that people would be able to hear no matter where they were seated in the chapel. They included meeting space for small groups and a place to prepare a cup of coffee.

They included plans for a gift shop where, for the first time, guests would be able to buy a candle made by Brother Jim, or a painting from the heart of Brother Antony, or notecards designed by the Printer Monk Father Mike. They offered not only space, but also their gifts and talents.

The monks have a life together, but they have chosen to care for others on a daily basis just as they care for themselves. To do so is to be human. As we wash our bodies and fold our clothing and shovel the driveway, we indicate that we have accepted our role and life, as it exists. We are making peace with ourselves and all the others around us.

When we fail to brush our teeth, wash our feet, and get enough sleep, we are heading for detachment from the real self and from others; we are folding in on ourselves. A person who is disconnecting from life will usually have symptoms of depression and addictive behaviors. It is also common for them to stop taking care of themselves. They skip a shower, don't brush their teeth or change their socks, and have a hard time finding a shirt and trousers that are matched and neat.

Attention to the details is a way to prepare a place for others. There is no one who does this better at St.

Benedict Monastery than Brother John Martin. John Martin and Lonni are good friends, and through the years she has come to appreciate his knack for lining up all the ducks in a row. He is careful when he prepares for liturgies. When he is given the task of developing the new community psalter, he takes every detail very seriously. And if you should be fortunate enough to go on vacation with him, he will also prepare thoroughly for that.

At John Martin's solemn profession, Lonni met a friend of his who had once taken a vacation with him. The man was single and a bit older than John Martin. He told her how John Martin had every day planned, and would pull out his list whenever they tried to figure out what came next. He did not object to spontaneity, but if he had a plan and it was a good plan, you stuck to it. After all, John Martin had laid out the plan for your vacation enjoyment. He had prepared a place for you.

Preparing a place says "welcome" and "you are accepted and honored." Few can resist such a welcome. In all our preparations for the other who comes to us, we will end up a little surprised. As we do the work of preparation, we prepare ourselves too and, something more, we are prepared by the divine presence. The work of preparation opens us up. We begin consciously to turn our will toward receiving others.

The work can be as simple as washing sheets for the guest room, baking a cake for the family who just lost their grandmother, or gathering wildflowers to put on the family table. You can paint a room at the homeless shelter. You can teach someone how to change the oil in her car.

Set an extra place at your table tonight and receive God who comes among us. Light a candle and take a deep breath and receive the presence of the One who is always with you. Remember this: There is a place prepared for you. It is a place where you can rest. It is a place where you are renewed and changed.

The work you do that prepares a home or a building or a yard to welcome others is very important work. It is holy work. But it is not the most important work of preparation. The most important work is preparing yourself to receive others. Only you know what you need to do to make that happen. Is there someone to forgive? Is there someone to release? Is there a fear to abandon? Is there an attitude to adjust?

We all have weapons to lie down and battles to call off before we can open up our hearts. It is a stance of surrender that we are talking about. Ultimately, hospitality is not about the table you set, or the driveway you plow. Hospitality is about preparing the holiest of holies. It is about the heart you make ready. Yours.

six

Companionship and Intimacy

here is one point we have to get very clear if we're going to be a person of love. There are zillions of degrees of intimacy in relationships. Even within a single relationship, the degree of intimacy will vary from week to week and year to year. This is important to remember, if we are going to avoid our feelings being trampled on constantly and our expectations frustrated.

Hospitality ultimately involves us with others, and we will become tangled up in relationships. We need to be aware that each of these relationships will be different from the next and will vary in degrees of closeness. But intimacy is the goal of hospitality, and in order to understand that, we need to look at the meaning of *intimacy* and *companionship*. We no longer have clear definitions of these words.

Having said there are degrees of intimacy we want to focus on two kinds of relating: intimacy and companionship. We realize that within these two categories there are shades and degrees of closeness. All of us get confused about how much we should reveal in a relationship, how much we should give, and how much we should let someone give us. Confusion is inevitable since we are daily bludgeoned with messages that tell us emotionally, spiritually healthy people *always* connect to others in a profound way.

Are we cold and heartless because we do not want to be intimate with every single person who crosses our paths? No. It isn't possible to achieve such a thing. We will have some very close relationships and we will have companionable ones. The media gives us the wrong idea about less intense relationships. They tell us that any relationship that is not intimate is unimportant, and so we have dismissed less-than-intimate relationships.

This is dangerous. We need relationships of depth, but we also need companionable relationships in which we listen to the other, show that we care, and are present to another person, even when tired or cranky. This kind of companionship is a healing thing for both the giver and the receiver, but it is not easy. It means we put our own feelings aside. Sounds easy until we have to do it.

Every relationship does *not* have to involve gut-level sharing. It is a beautiful thing to simply respond to others' everyday, simple needs. Reassure someone that they are stronger than they know. Include the shy person in the conversation. Notice the well-executed report or talk. Offer a cup of tea to someone who looks tired.

Maybe someone just needs to be left alone. Listen when people talk. It is impossible to exaggerate the number of people who never feel heard, even by friends, family, or spouse. Being a person of hospitality involves getting out of myself for long enough periods that I can hear other people, really hear them, and pay attention to what they might need at this moment.

Some people are very good at this; it seems to come naturally. The rest of us have to work at it. Father Dan has often said that Brother Benedict, the oldest of the monks in his community has been his companion for forty years and he has felt this companionship deeply.

Yet they have never sat down and had what we would call a "heart-to-heart." Brother Benedict is profoundly present to people without even trying. If you asked him how he has managed such a thing, he would not even know what you are talking about. His life of prayer has poured a hospitable spirit into him.

"He is a constant presence to me," Father Dan says. "Even though we have talked about deep and serious things, we haven't told each other our stories. But he is sensitive to what I feel; I have tried to emulate this in him."

Emulating someone is a good way to learn hospitality. Find a hospitable person and spend time with them. Listen to them. Do not look for methods or tips from them. Just be together and you will be astonished at what happens.

In Benedict's entire adulthood, this holy old man has probably never had what anyone else would consider an intimate relationship. He is kind and good to all, and people love him. Recently he was in the hospital. Father Dan said he couldn't help noticing how all the nurses fell in love with the old monk. When he visited, they would tell him what a kind and sweet man Brother Ben is; they fell over each other to take care of him.

"I know Brother Benedict and he did nothing out of the ordinary," Dan said. "He was just himself, sometimes sweet, sometimes grumpy, sometimes bewildered, but always real. I took him home from the hospital and told him some of the very nice things the nurses had said about him. He waved it off and said, 'Oh, they say that about everyone.'"

Brother Ben is an excellent companion, not just to the monks, but to anyone God places in his life that day. He is almost completely deaf. This makes it hard for him to get to know the people who come to the monastery for mass on Sunday or during the week. Yet, when he was sick, there was an outpouring of concern for him because people cared about him. They had felt his love for all of them without ever having a single intimate moment with him.

Since he's recovered, he has become the most popular monk with the Sunday crowd. During the passing of the peace people jam to be with him. He sits in the very front of the chapel, and he just turns and touches hands and smiles and makes a sign of peace at people. Father Dan says he thinks of it as his Jay Leno imitation. They all want a piece of him and he gives the best he can.

Through the years, Father Dan has observed instances when he can tell, at a gut level, that Brother Ben cares deeply. It is unmistakable. He reveals his caring in a comment, or a pat on the back, or a joke. His deep, companionable nature has been easier for Dan to receive and cherish than the efforts other monks have made at intimacy, before a relationship has grown to the point that intimacy happens naturally.

Whether you have been married or not, you may have noticed that marriage and even close friendships are similar to Brother Ben's way of companionship. Marriage has moments of intimacy, but for the most part, operates on a companionable level day to day. There are kids to bathe, dogs to clip, and groceries to fetch. Someone has to rake the leaves and someone has to get the cat off the roof. There is no time for intimate discussions while little Tommy is fingerpainting on the guestroom walls.

There was a morning drive-time show in Flint, Michigan, that asked callers to talk about what made a marriage work. As you'd expect, they received many calls about communication and romance and telling the other person what you enjoy sexually. Each of these callers thought they had the one answer to the big question. Someone suggested a date night. Someone suggested a fantasy night. All fine ideas—if you can pull it off. Most married people can't; life just doesn't happen that way.

It was one of the disk jockeys that, in the end, said the most sensible and reassuring thing of all. He said, "You have to be able to look across the room, after the kid has trashed it, and you're scrubbing the rug while your mate is wiping grape jelly off the kid's face and think, Dear God, I am so happy. I can sit with her and do nothing. I can dance with her on the deck under the stars in our backyard. I can tell her my wildest dream and she won't laugh out loud. She doesn't even care that I watch football. This is great, even though it isn't what I expected. It's better than that."

Companionship is the great gift of marriage. Intimacy does not happen from the first cup of coffee until the light goes off at night. Such a thing would just be too much. Too often, we have too many unrealistic expectations of marriage, and they spill over into our other relationships.

Doing life together, as monks and married couples do, provides an anchor of stability. Most relationships today are less stable than they were fifty years ago.

Families are no longer held together by economic security, religious tradition, and cultural expectations, and
the extended family has a lesser role in the lives of most
couples. Most people experience the shattering of family ties, if not personally, then within their closest
sphere of family and friends.

Just as a monastic community creates a shelter for
others, a couple creates a life-giving shelter when their
union is a healthy and loving one. Love, by its nature,
is life-giving. This does not mean that all couples
become parents; producing children is not essential to
loving each other. A couple creates a family, and if not
biologically, then they do so in other ways. When a
couple doesn't love well enough to open their borders
and, out of the strength of their love, welcome others,
the union will collapse on itself and become destructive. The same is true in the monastery.

No matter how intimate a relationship might be,
that single relationship is not enough to satisfy the
human hunger for love. No human being has enough
love to meet such needs. Only our passion for God is
enough love; only God's passion for us can make us
whole. Most of us will have intimate relationships,
but we make a mistake if we think that intimacy is all

we need. We also need companions, we need good fun, we need the brief and tender moment when a stranger stoops to help collect the clutter that has dropped to the floor. Moments like these help us remember that the universe is a safe place. We come fully awake.

Benedict knew there would always be strangers, guests, and visitors knocking on our door. He knew people would always show up to escape the chaos and find a moment or two of quiet. He understood that people are looking for a sanctuary. Marriage and intimate relationships are safe places where you can relax and let down the pretenses. We all need such places. Benedict tells his monks to make the monastery such a place. Even the daily reality of intimate relationships may not feel intimate a lot of the time. But the support and strength of intimacy will be there when you need it if the relationship is solid and both people are capable of intimate bonding.

Intimacy does not consist of a constant level of relating; instead, it simply happens when it needs to if people are open and able to enter the moment. Many years ago, while Father Dan was serving the Detroit parish, he received a call that one of the parish families had just had a terrible tragedy. Their eldest son had taken his own life.

In the days following the young man's death, Father Dan visited their home. He had not been close to the family. He knew them, but they were not friends. He watched as the mother become inconsolable and the father lost himself in a drunken stupor.

He could not imagine the pain this couple was feeling. He did not judge the couple for how they were handling their son's death. None of us know what we would do if such a thing happened. They had no room inside them for anything but the pain. The boy was not the only child in the family, however; they also had a little girl, five or six years old.

Dan remembers, "I went over to check on the family and found the mother locked in her bedroom and the father sitting in a chair, completely intoxicated and basically unconscious. The little girl was sitting on the floor sobbing, with her frail little shoulders heaving and her eyes red from so much crying that you wondered if her little body could handle the force of all the pain. She was completely alone in her grief, not because her parents were cruel or uncaring, but because they were shattered.

"I picked up the child, and without saying a word, put her on my lap and sat in a rocking chair. I held her and rocked while she cried for a couple of hours. A bond formed between us instantly."

Dan did not become a friend of the family. Once they had come through the crisis he was again just a parish priest. Yet he shared with that little girl one of the most profoundly intimate connections he can ever remember. He lost all thought of himself. There was an understanding between them that was beyond words.

Mutual reverence and not warm, fuzzy, social comforts is the climate of Benedictine hospitality. We have lost completely the awareness that relationships come in degrees. We don't know how to move from casual to intimate and back again. We have forgotten that we ought to pour ourselves out sometimes, and hold back at other times.

Not every guest is an angel and neither is every monk. Discretion requires you to respect someone without trying to be their best friend. Hospitality is not a call to unquestioning intimacy with the whole world. Monks are not flower children, and the monastery meal is not a love-in. Hospitality is a call to revere what is sacred in every person ever born. While intimacy does not have to happen in every instance of hospitality, reverence does. We reverence people not because they are pleasant, but because God is present in them.

Intimacy is what we want and what we fear most. A major problem with any discussion about intimacy is that the word itself is confusing and the meaning of intimacy is relative. Intimacy happens in companionable relationships, and companionship happens in intimate relationships.

Equating sex with intimacy contributes to our misunderstanding the true nature of intimacy. If a couple has had sex we call it being intimate. When people discuss their dating relationships, sometimes they ask, "Have you been intimate?" They mean, have you had sex yet? We call women's lingerie "intimate apparel." It is no wonder that we do not know the meaning of intimacy.

In reporting an acquaintance-rape situation one news reporter stated, "He had been intimate with her for six months." Sex does not automatically create intimacy, as millions of people have painfully discovered. In making sex and intimacy one and the same, intimacy has been belittled while an entire set of faulty expectations of casual sex has been created. When we confuse intimacy with sexual relations, we imply that sex is the only means to closeness, and we devalue the growing together that two people need to do before they become sexually involved.

To imply that our deepest needs are met only by sexual encounters has set up an entire generation to be disillusioned. Sex can happen between two people who don't even like each other. It can be used as a weapon and as a reward system. People can be demeaned by sex. Sex can be beautiful and make you a better person, or it can crush you. Intimacy, however, never crushes the human soul; it only builds it up. Because intimacy regards the other as valuable and cherished, it makes us more human.

Dozens of relationships involve intimacy, including parental and family ones. To make intimacy explicitly sexual is to suggest that these closest relationships are less than intimate. When I experience genuine intimacy, I know to the bone that I am not alone. This knowing comes through relationship. It is not a thing I realize with my brain, but a thing I discover with my heart. Intimacy feels familiar, yet sometimes the deep sustaining power of intimacy jolts your sleepy heart wide awake and everything becomes brighter and better.

Intimacy is the deep experience of knowing another human heart.

The right kind of sex is certainly intimate, but we must not forget that sex happens without intimacy all the time. By confusing sex and intimacy, we use sex in the hope of experiencing intimacy. To be intimate is to be figuratively naked, without walls, completely open to another human being. That sort of intimacy makes for wonderful sex.

In our culture the attraction of sex is excitement and pleasure, but most people are craving to be known when they have sex, even if they don't understand the primal drives that compel them toward others in sexual union.

Without intimacy, sex only deepens abiding and severe loneliness. The purpose of sex is to enhance an already intimate relationship; when we use it for any other purpose it fails us. Our bodies are linked to who we are, after all; we cannot exist in this life without a body. What you do to my body you do to me. This makes casual sex devastating. Sex means something, it says something. Casual sex lies. Faithless sex, based on nothing but the urge to mate, is a violation of my person—it is definitely not intimacy.

Lyrics to a recent rock song proclaimed, "When everything's made to be broken, I just want you to know who I am. . . ." This is a cry for intimacy. Another song says, "I don't know if I've ever been touched by a hand that loves me." When a gifted songwriter lets you into his or her inner regions, you hear in their music the human heart crying for intimacy rather than sex.

When people talk about romantic relationships, they often leave unsaid their desire to be known, to connect. Often, what appears to be about sex is actually about intimacy.

Intimacy has also come to mean *personal*. We see a couple of close friends talking and think, "I won't interrupt an intimate moment." We think of secrets as intimate, and associate them with the private and personal. In using the language in this way, we further muddy the meaning of intimacy and relegate intimacy to the most private realms of human experience. We don't make room for intimacy in companionable kinds of relationships or in the everyday events of our lives, in the way we welcome others and open our hearts to them.

Intimacy is the experience of sharing life together. When Father Dan talks about his relationship with

Brother Ben he is speaking out of a lifetime shared. But intimacy happens in other ways.

Intimacy happened in America when every American we knew was sitting in front of a television watching the events of September 11 unfold.

We suddenly felt connected to a bigger whole that consists of all of us from sea to shining sea. We experienced a brief period of knowing we are part of one another and we belong to each other. That was an experience of intimacy we shared with strangers, the people next door, and our best friends.

You may remember the night the CEO of a big financial firm that had been housed in the World Trade Center sobbed on television and said, "I went home and kissed my children. . . ." That same night Lonni was at her family cabin in the woods. She remembers stepping outside at 7:00 P.M. and lighting a candle on the porch, along with millions of other Americans. Then she sat on the steps and tried to pray but couldn't. Like the guy on television the only noises her soul could make were uncontrolled sobs. We were together in that, all of us hardly able to do anything but weep.

We gathered to watch the memorial service from the National Cathedral and listened to Billy Graham say in a faltering voice, " I am an old man now. The older I get, the more I cling to hope." And we all clung to hope together.

We watched when the lights on Broadway came back on. Matthew Broderick said, "It's dark right now, but tonight the lights are on again." The same night Nathan Lane said, "You can't dim the joy in this country." Joy isn't a word you hear people use very often. The actor was on to something. Genuine joy doesn't usually happen until you've been to the depths of despair. It is not like happiness. Joy is the internal passion that remains after the best attempts of evil to knock the life out of you. If America has ever had a chance to realize real joy, this is it.

You might remember the volunteer firefighters. One who had gone to New York within days of the attack talked about what it was like for him to be at Ground Zero. He was a big man with a ponytail and a red kerchief tied around his head. He looked like his nose had been broken a couple times. He was the kind of guy you cross the street to avoid. There he was, on national television, with tears streaming down his face as he said, "We are all family now. I love everyone."

Next week he might be singing, "Are you ready for some football?" but that day he looked toward heaven and whispered, "We are going to be crying for a long time." We never expected to have a place in America we would call Ground Zero, and if that is not enough to make a tough guy cry, nothing could.

Father Dan was in Rome, on community business, on September 11. He was there with one other American monk, Father Livy, his traveling companion and a brother monk from Detroit. While the two men have belonged to the same congregation and have known each other for decades, they don't have an intimate friendship. Yet when the attacks happened, Dan recalled feeling suddenly connected to the only other American there and being glad he was with him. It had been incredibly difficult to be away from America during that period, but no one could return until air space was opened up again.

Dan remembers going through customs when he returned to the United States. "The customs official looked at my papers and said something about I must have been in Rome on church business. I nodded, and then he looked me in the eye and said, 'Welcome home, Father.' Customs officials had never said that before. I wanted to hug him. Everything had changed."

All these months later, it is easy to be cynical and question the sincerity, or importance, of the connection we all felt to one another in the immediate days and weeks following the New York and Pentagon attacks. For the most part, Americans are back to being Marlboro men and women and pumping up our own importance and independence to an unreasonable extent.

But that's how intimacy works. It happens when we least expect it, and it shows up in odd situations between strangers. It makes strangers into brothers and sisters. It flares up and gives us an emotional rush of acceptance and belonging and being known, and then it ebbs away, always there to wash over us when we need a shoulder to lean on, a hand to clutch, or a joke that will make us laugh all the way to our toes.

Among the most unforgettable images that have emerged from the American tragedy is the number of people who called home with their last breath. Whether they called from the fifty-second floor of the World Trade Center or from a hijacked plane they used their last breath to say, "I love you. Whatever happens, remember the love." To say, " I love . . . " is an affirmation of life at its highest and holiest. To say, "I love . . . "

is to say, "I live, I am human, and you have made me more human. I will always live in you who love me."

Lonni and her husband, David, lost a good friend in the days just before September 11. They had known him a long time. David went to high school with his wife. The two couples had taken country-and-western dance classes together. Lonni says that Joe was a lot like Brother Ben.

"He was one of those people who could make you feel like the only person in the room when he talked to you. Yet he wasn't the kind to make an effort at intimacy. He didn't wake up in the morning and say, 'Today I am going to bond intimately with other people.' He just got out of bed and spent his days making other people feel like they mattered."

He was part of a service club, and whenever the club got off course and more interested in socializing than service, Joe was one of the people who would kick them back on track again. As his diabetes stole his sight, he would make jokes about being a blind guy. His disability never kept him from living with a great deal of joy and enthusiasm.

If you had asked Joe about the meaning of intimacy, he would have looked at you with bewilderment. An answer would have failed him. But then he would have poured another cup of coffee, he would have taken you bowling or told you a joke, and you would leave him feeling taller, stronger, and more human.

Lonni's husband, a United Methodist minister, officiated at the funeral for Joe. At the end of it he said, "Go and serve the way Joe served. Go and put joy in the life of others the way Joe did. Go and love the way Joe loved."

This is the message from the people who called from the heights that were about to crash down around all of us and change our world forever: "Go and love in memory of me." This is the message of Benedict to his monks: "Live and love in the name of Jesus."

The ancient monk Benedict must have known that his celibate monks would discover the magic of intimacy, not only in each other, but in the stranger at the door. So he told them to keep the door open, and greet the stranger as if you are greeting God.

Benedict is sane and sensible about the whole thing. He tells his monks to greet the guests and honor the guests and then get back to what you were doing. Hospitality thrives in the monastery because every single day there is someone to love and the recklessly open heart of the monk is available. He may do no more than smile at you, or hold your hand for a second, but he is giving you what he has in the present moment to give you.

In the end, intimacy and companionship are different shades of the same color, and perhaps the distinctions we draw are false. What matters is that we open ourselves up, and we love. What matters is that we love, every single gorgeous second we get a chance at it.

seven

The Making
of a Heart—
It's Not Easy to Love

It just isn't easy to love. People disappoint us when they are doing the best they can. None of us starts out in life mature, and none of us is automatically good at loving. It does seem that some are better at it, naturally, than others. If we really look into their lives, we discover some special contributing factor that accounts for what seems like their "natural" ability to love. They may have helped care for their grandparents, or had a handicapped sibling. Firstborn of large families tend to be especially nurturing. We need other people to help us grow. Sometimes it is the one who is most difficult to be around that we need the most. Sometimes we are the most difficult to be around, and then we need grace and acceptance. Without the defying and difficult presence of others, we would not try as hard, because we would not have to. It is an inescapable reality that our relationships are the soil from which we grow a heart capable of caring.

Father Michael Green joined the monastery one year after Father Dan. They both grew up in Detroit and both went to the Benedictine high school. They knew each other in high school, casually. Their lives were both deeply touched by the monks, and forty years ago each of these young men left their home and family to go to St. Benedict Monastery.

Dan is a year older than Mike. When the monastic community decided they needed these two young men to become priests, Dan went to Toronto to study theology a year before he was joined by Mike. Father Mike likes to say they actually majored in hockey.

While in Toronto, Father Dan started getting involved with teen ministry. He says he didn't know that the kids liked him. He was a quiet young man— not the kind of youth minister to wear orange pants, put a plant on his head, and dance on the table. At the end of his education, Dan returned home to Michigan for his ordination and first mass. He was shocked—and delighted—when seven cars full of teens from Toronto showed up to celebrate his ordination. A celebration followed the great event. The events around his ordination were naturally very special to the newly ordained priest; he cherished that memory.

Something happened in Father Dan when those teenagers showed up. It revealed to him, in an undeniable way, that God was with him as he worked with youth. It confirmed his gift, and when our gifts and graces are confirmed we feel affirmed as a human being. That kind of thing is very special and we want to hold onto such an experience. We want to lock it in time and make it a defining moment.

His friend Mike was there, too. Father Mike is a gregarious kind of guy; he kisses all the women and babies in a room. One friend of Dan's says Father Mike reminds him of Tigger; you know Tigger, companion to Winnie the Pooh, who is "bouncy, trouncy . . . full of fun, fun, fun." That would be Father Mike. Whatever he does, he does with enthusiasm.

Lonni was his dance partner at a square dance a few years ago. If you've ever square danced, you know there is a move where the guy releases the woman's hand to another partner. It's a swing release kind of movement. He is supposed to release her and sort of step aside, then she moves in line with her next partner. It is intended to be a smooth move. Lonni said when she danced with Father Mike, it was more like being "launched" than released; she called it a "swing launch" due to the energy and enthusiasm of Father Mike. Full of fun, fun, fun.

One year after Dan's ordination, it was time for Mike to be ordained. Remember, there had been a celebration only a year previously during which Mike had become acquainted with Dan's young friends. For Father Mike, any friend of Father Dan's was a friend of his. It had been a lot of fun, and connections had been forged, so it was natural that Mike invited some of those young people to his party as well. It would also be their chance to see Father Dan again.

"I was furious," Dan recalls. "They were my friends, not his friends. How dare he invite *my* friends to his party? How dare he assume that would be fine with me—he did not even talk to me about it. In my anger, I wrote a letter to Mike. I told him to get his own friends. I told him he had no right to invite my friends. I said things I'm deeply ashamed of saying. I wrote the letter, shoved it under his door, and did I ever feel better. For a little while anyway."

Dan did not sleep much that night. By morning he was horrified at what he done. He was awake while Mike slept, peacefully happy with the events of the day. Dan could not believe he had given in to jealousy and pride. He couldn't believe he had said such awful things to his faithful friend. He was disgusted with himself.

Very early in the morning, after Dan had fallen into an exhausted sleep, Mike slipped the envelope back under Dan's door.

"He did an amazing thing. He returned the letter and wrote on the envelope, 'Dan, this isn't you.' It was the response I needed most, but could never have expected. He didn't just forgive me. He erased it and gave me the benefit of any doubt and he moved on, before we even discussed it. He actually did not even need to discuss it."

It was more grace than the young priest could have hoped for, and it has stuck with him all these years. When he thinks of the times he most needed grace, he most needed to be understood and forgiven, he remembers that one incident with Mike Green, one of his oldest and best friends. Because Father Dan knows there are times when something that is less "real" in him sticks up its head, he is very understanding when it happens to other people.

His ability to understand is the product of monasticism. The life of the monks makes it difficult to avoid themselves. All that silence, solitude, and prayer puts you up close with who you really are. Living day after day with the same people you argued with last week and celebrated with last year—people who know your story—will keep your ideas about yourself in perspective. Sure, people can avoid themselves in monastic life. Any monk can tell you a story about how he has avoided himself and has seen others do it also. But their life in common, relentlessly in common, makes it tough to live out a pattern of self-avoidance.

All of us are hard to like and even harder to love sometimes. The human person is capable of great loyalty and great betrayal. One single, remarkable soul can house huge contradictions. You can't tell on the outside what is going on inside. From the moment we slip from the womb we begin the journey of becoming who we are. Even the best of childhoods traumatize our fragile souls and we learn to cover up and compensate.

We learn to clutch what is ours and we learn to mistrust others.

There is always the real you. The one with the potential. The one you dream of becoming. The one you are in your best moments.

As we grow spiritually, we recover this original identity and shed the many layers of the false self. This growth is an important part of spirituality.

Understand that when we refer to a "false" self we are not promoting denial, and we are not suggesting that we are anything less than fully responsible for our worst moments. There is no bad twin to blame when we behave something less than human. It was not Father Dan's alter ego who wrote the nasty letter to his friend. But that action did emerge from a part of Dan that is fundamentally *not* the person he is becoming. Failure is not the final word, however. Even if we know that on an intellectual level, having someone affirm it the way Father Mike did for Father Dan helps tremendously.

You are becoming something. You are becoming more patient, more loving, more angry, more selfish—there is some fundamental person at the root of it all. It may be a person of love, or a person of selfish indifference. Every day we make choices that take us toward becoming one or the other. We probably make most of our choices in favor of loving. It is rare to meet a person who makes all of their choices in favor of loving.

Hospitality is a way to help others discover their true selves. They need to see that precious person reflected in your eyes sometimes, before they can believe it for themselves. It is no easy thing to give this to other people. We know that. We can force ourselves, through gritted teeth and clenched spirits, to be gracious to the one who needs a second chance. Not much reward in it for us, but we know we can do it. We can let down our resistance and let acceptance happen naturally. It is better both for us and for the person. Our ability to accept others begins with whether or not we are in touch with our dark side. As we have said, monks live with themselves without blinking at the dark side, and this is what allows them to be as accepting as they are. They are able to accept strangers without expecting them to be perfect.

You might remember a biblical story about a woman caught in adultery. Jesus tells the men who are about to stone her that the one who is without sin (and the Greek actually says "without this sin"—adultery) should toss the first stone. And he doesn't get any takers.

A realistic understanding of the self allows us to better accept others. If we can forgive ourselves, we become better at forgiving others. When we have searched hard for the best that is inside of ourselves, it becomes easier to find the best in others.

Gratitude is an appropriate response once you know who you really are. Gratitude for all the grace that overlooks the worst, while moving you toward your original best self. Gratitude makes it easier to handle all the hard-to-like people who will step into your path.

Lonni's youngest daughter, Andrea, was in an auto accident just before her seventeenth birthday. It was a near-fatal accident. Lonni has never forgotten sitting with Andrea in the intensive care unit, watching her chest move up and down, praying for every single breath. Lonni thought of Andrea when she met a woman on an airplane who had been in an auto accident.

The woman was older than Andrea, and it appeared that her injuries were not as extensive. Her face had sustained a lot of damage, however. She wore the scars not only from the accident, but also from numerous reconstructive surgeries. Generally Lonni reads or sleeps on flights; she does not make small talk with other passengers.

"This woman was determined to tell me her story," Lonni remembers, but Lonni did not want to listen. It was not a pretty story. The woman was angry and bitter. She had lost her face and no amount of surgery was going to give it back to her. She bragged about the Mercedes she bought with the insurance settlement money; she spoke of how "she's set for life" now. She even said that she has all the male attention she wants, despite being "ugly as sin" because she could always buy another "boy toy."

Not liking the direction of the conversation, Lonni told her about her daughter and brought up the subject of anger and how people worked through anger after such a tragedy. It was not something the other woman wanted to discuss. Lonni did not want to be sitting next to her, and she did not like the woman.

In a similar situation, before Andrea's accident, Lonni would have buried her nose in the book she was reading and not looked up, regardless of the woman's fervent attempts to attract her attention. She thought hospitality did not include listening to annoying strangers on airplanes. "I didn't have time for rude, angry people," she said.

What made the difference? Gratitude. Lonni's daughter had been spared. Yes, she was an angry young woman sometimes, but every day she was growing stronger and learning to release her anger. Andrea was alive. Andrea was on a course toward healing and dealing with her rage. Lonni felt a huge sense of gratitude for this. She knew it could be different, but they had been spared so much. Lonni had friends whose seventeen-year-old daughter had died in a car crash only a few years before. But Andrea would make it.

The woman next to Lonni? Well, it was anyone's guess whether or not she would ever truly recover from the accident. And no amount of expensive cars or casual sex would change that reality. Not only did Lonni wonder if the woman next to her would ever be a whole person, she wondered if there was anyone in the whole world who cared. The woman didn't talk of family or friends—only things and people to be used.

What did it really cost Lonni to listen to the woman? It was such a little thing and it seemed that not many people had ever taken the time to do it. That was understandable; she was difficult to be around because she was self-centered, loud, and intent on being noticed. Without gratitude for her own daughter's life, Lonni would have ignored the woman.

Gratitude is at the center of a hospitable heart. It keeps everything in perspective. Often we allow day after gifted day to come and go without one sigh of gratitude for the beauty of it all. We don't slow our breath to hear the song of the wind, or taste the miracle of an apple. We take for granted the health of the little ones who sleep in their beds, and we assume the one who loves me today will be here to love me again tomorrow. What an arrogant life we lead.

Perhaps you recall being thirteen and having someone tell you that you ought to be grateful that you have shoes because some people have no feet. Perhaps you recall being six and having your grandfather tell you that you ought to be grateful for liver and onions because some children went to bed hungry. You know, it did not make you feel grateful. Knowing you should feel gratitude feels awful. It made you feel rotten. Guilty. Like dirt.

We know we ought to be grateful for every sunrise. We ought to be grateful for every bite of food. We ought to be grateful for every heart that has ever loved us. We ought to be grateful for every starry night. All of life is a resounding call to gratitude, and until we honestly feel the joy of gratitude, giving will be difficult for us. Gratitude is the best feeling you will ever have. But you can't feel grateful just because you ought to.

Gratitude is what you feel on the perfect summer day with the wind in your face and the sun on your shoulder, as the laughter of someone you love kisses your ear. Try as hard as you know how, and still you can't do more than muster up a sense that yes, you ought to be grateful. You really cannot make it happen; gratitude, like faith, is given to you. It springs on you. It knocks the wind out of you just when everything seemed impossible.

Anxiety makes you ready for gratitude. So does having enough courage not to dull the anxiety with alcohol, or spending, or eating, or whatever your usual escape might be. Shut the door, experience the anxiety, and you are ready for gratitude. You can't control gratitude or make it happen, regardless of what your mother told you. Try to force gratitude and you end up with guilt instead.

Gratitude happens most often during suffering, loss, and other really hard stuff. It is the leading edge of joy. It happens when the big reality hits you. You have no more right to be loved than anyone else. Your job is a fluke. Your children have no more right to health and security than the children in Bosnia. Your friends are not obligated to put up with you. Your education—well, consider yourself fortunate you were not born into the poverty of Calcutta. It is all a gift. Every single molecule, every smile, every taste of sunshine, is a gift.

Gratitude opens up space inside of us for others. There is less of me in me when I am grateful. I can see that you, too, are a gift to me. Even if you aren't easy to be around.

There was a monk who lived with Father Dan at the monastery for many years. He is gone now, no longer a monk, but during his stay he was the most difficult to live with of any monk, or any person, Father Dan had ever known.

The monk took no responsibility for his actions, his emotions, or his boatload of dysfunction. Plus, he never got the idea of community. If something went wrong, he pointed out how it was someone else's fault. He left little doubt that he was out solely for himself. He did no more than he had to do. If he was sweeping the kitchen and you asked him to sweep the pantry too, he would say, "It isn't my job to sweep the pantry." He was the kind who took the last piece of apple pie without asking if anyone would like to share it with him. He was suspicious of all the monks, saying that some of them went into his room when he was away and took things from him.

Day after day, Dan looked across the table at this annoying man and faced the reality of looking across the table at him for the rest of his life. How can we be anything but a stranger to someone so thoroughly impossible to like?

Dan says he never did learn to like the monk, but once he became Prior he had the sacred responsibility to look after the monk's growth. He encouraged him to become involved with needy people. Father Dan hoped that compassion would incite growth. He encouraged him to use his gifts to work with others. Dan insisted that the monk try new things and attempt to open his mind to new possibilities. Dan persevered in his attempts to find the real person behind all the negativity. It was a difficult situation for both Prior and monk. But the man seemed to be in love with his own destruction. He refused to listen, and above all a monk must listen.

"I can get along with almost anyone. I have never been more challenged to accept someone than I was with that particular monk," Father Dan remembers. He admits that frequently monks struggle to understand and accept each other; it does not happen automatically. Perseverance with the unlovable one will often hold you until a breakthrough occurs. Sometimes, however, the breakthrough never comes. It never came with the monk, and he eventually left.

Dan knows, however, that it was good for him, personally, to struggle and keep trying. He had no way to avoid the man and had to be open to the notion that God had brought them both to the monastery at the same time to live a shared life.

We all have rough edges that need some sanding down. Everyone is a bag of contradictions. Usually we are not in such bad shape emotionally that others flee from us, but we are still contrary and difficult sometimes. Trying to find the good in others, and working with them to reveal it, helps soften us around the edges.

What is the secret of people who seem always to feel grateful without being prompted, people who keep looking for the good in others, people who welcome others even when it is hard to do?

The secret is, these people have courage. Courage takes us past thinking and talking about hospitality into the realm of the will. Courage is the power of the heart, and it resides not in the emotion, but in the will and the power to choose. Courageous people *will* themselves to move past an obstacle that paralyzes others.

Remember *The Wizard of Oz?*

It is the story of Dorothy, who is trying to get home. Dorothy does not lack courage. She's lost, but she is not cowardly. The Tin Man thinks he lacks a heart, and the Scarecrow thinks he lacks a brain, and the Cowardly Lion thinks he lacks courage—only the Lion is right; what they all lack, we eventually find out, is courage. They lack the courage to become more than they are. They lack the courage to get through the tough times, and when they stand in the hall of mirrors and smoke and roaring voices they lack the courage to declare themselves—all except the little girl, who has come this far by courage, and will make it home by courage.

One day Father Mike was working on the monastery computers with a friend when a rude and uninvited visitor showed up. It was during the period that the monastery's chapel was under construction. They had been at work for a couple hours when a young man suddenly walked into the room. Father Mike asked him who he was and what he wanted.

The man told Mike that the person who was using the scaffolding outside had rented it from him, and had not made payments, and so he was there to take it down and take it home. He that he had called the guy's wife and the guy's mother, and no one was giving him any satisfaction. As he talked, the visitor grew more agitated. His hands hung clenched at his sides. He was taking on the appearance of someone looking for a fight.

"No one screws me," he said loudly, as if it were Father Mike who owed him for the scaffolding. Mike suggested they talk about it in the hallway. He wanted to make sure his friend was out of the line of fire if things got out of hand. The man just continued to rant, finally saying, "I am going to take the scaffolding and you can't stop me!"

Father Mike replied, "I'm not going to try and stop you, but neither am I giving you permission to take it. All I've heard is your side of the story, and there is bound to be more to it than what you have told me. If you have decided you are taking the scaffolding, then just go do it, but remember, I am not allowing you to take it. You are removing it from our property without my permission."

Mike was firm and clear. He kept his voice low and he looked the man in the eye steadily. He refrained from matching the man anger for anger, insult for insult. His was the voice of reason.

Despite Mike's concern for the monastery and the person with him, despite his anxiety over what this man might do next, Mike kept a cool head. He was not intimidated by the huff and gruff of a bully. He knew that what stood before him was a scared little man making a lot of noise, bellowing and blowing hot air.

Father Mike was courageous. He did not back down. He did not give in. He did not compromise. He remained respectful while being appropriately strong. His calm, steady reply drained the hot air from the unexpected visitor. When Mike finished, the man stood there a moment, his legs apart, his arms folded in a defensive stance. He said again.

"You can't stop me."

Mike paused and said, "I'm not trying to stop you."

The man turned and left the room. He had come looking for a fight. He was so angry with the man to whom he had rented the equipment that he arrived on the work site ready to do battle. He was set to fight the first person he encountered. But Father Mike did not need to do battle. He had nothing to prove.

It is important that we not allow people to drag us into their fights with the world. We have to stay on the outside of the situation and attempt to discern what is really happening. Do they want the problem resolved, or are they just looking for a fight? Father Mike acted well when trouble came knocking on the door. He risked looking like a fool for the sake of peace.

The difficult person comes with a mountain of emotion attached. The emotion itself can become the center of any relating that happens. We are not doing the person any good if we become caught up in their emotion and negativity.

If we center down into the quiet in our hearts, we can hear what is really happening. As we grow in meditation and prayer, we become better at resting in the center. When you are conscious of living every second gathered before the Divine you just do not rattle easily. Father Mike has spent over forty years at prayer. He has the ability to see who a person really is. He is able to discern what is actually happening in a certain situation.

When Dan tells us of how Mike forgave him because "that wasn't really you," and we hear of how Mike dealt with a confrontational hothead, we hear in both stories an ability to size up a situation and get to the heart of it, quickly. You aren't born with that ability. It comes only through years of paying attention to people, listening to them and hearing the sounds of a human heart being the most honest it knows how to be.

When you hear that sound, you don't forget it; you recognize it afterward every single time it happens. But you will not hear it at all if you don't pay attention to people. If I am the stranger attempting to be known, and there you are, not listening, will I keep trying? Probably not. As hard as it is, try to hear the one who is hard to love.

"Because how can we be other than strangers when at those rare moments of our lives when we stop hiding from each other and try instead passionately and profoundly to make ourselves known to each other, we find this is precisely what we cannot do?" wonders writer Frederick Buechner in *Telling Secrets*.

When we relate to a difficult person, we operate from a basic assumption: I need to protect myself. But to live the way of hospitality means extending grace to people. You cannot be hospitable and gracious from behind your high wall. If you live by grace you become helpful. You become accepting. Even when it is impossible to accept certain behaviors and impossible to like them, you accept them. The centrality of love insists that we give the hard-to-like a chance.

Of course the difficulty of loving is complicated. It is not only the hard-to-like that we have trouble accepting; it is everyone. It is just hard to love sometimes.

"I honestly want to be more open to people, but I face people and situations that make it impossible."

"Yes, I want to be more hospitable, but I see no reason why I should open up to people who will use me and be ungrateful for what they are given."

"I know that Jesus went around accepting people and associating with the outcasts, but Jesus didn't live in the world I live in."

"I would love you, but you really are not all that lovable."

But.

The word *but* is all about our doubts, our justifications, and our excuses. To stop accepting your own excuses is a very courageous act.

We need time and practice to grow in accepting the difficult people. We must try or it will never happen at all. Hidden at the heart of all Creation is an original goodness. If we live in the presence of the Divine through prayer and gratitude, if we live courageously, this goodness will reveal itself.

It is very hard to keep a straight face and say there is good in everyone. We have seen evidence to the contrary, haven't we? It is hard to believe, but we keep trying to prove that there is good in everyone. We know people don't always choose goodness. We only have to look in the mirror to be reminded of that.

Goodness, most of the time, seems like an impossible dream, and the quest to find it in others no more than the fantasy of children. But if we don't try to believe it, we will end up densely fatalistic and unable to see the most obvious good. It is worth the effort to believe.

We give each other another chance to make the right choice when we accept and forgive, even when it is very difficult. Hospitality to the unchosen goodness in others will come more easily if we are practicing with ourselves.

Our ability to care is more than we know. Prayer will expand it. Courage will expand it. Risk will expand it. Caring, the tiny little bit of it we can manage, will expand as we give ourselves more chances to say *yes* to others.

In the Disney animated movie, *Lion King*, there is a scene in which the adolescent Simba comes to the end of his running from himself. He has escaped, hidden, and taken on an attitude that nothing matters. As he is chased down by the truth about himself, his Father appears to him and says, "You are more than you have become."

Regardless of what you and I have become, regardless of what anyone has become—we are all created to be more. There is an unchosen goodness in us. It exists, whether or not we choose it. We must learn to make the choices that will make us more.

This is the Christian story, the dominant story that guides the Western world. Jesus always called people to more. He called them beyond their plans for themselves, beyond their religious convictions, beyond their conditions. We can call each other beyond our worst choices.

eight

Making Room
for Yourself

*I*t is impossible to address the topic of hospitality without considering an individual's rights and boundaries. In pop psychology the word boundaries is used to describe the lines we each draw to protect ourselves. Psychologists consistently agree that some boundaries are necessary for a full and healthy life.

A few years ago Lonni and her husband welcomed into their home a man who had just been released from prison. He was a friend of Lonni's brother, and he had nowhere else to go. The family he came from had not taught him to respect other people or to insist that others respect you. The real meaning of *boundaries* is the insistence that I will not be violated by your selfishness.

If he had any fragile sense of boundaries, prison destroyed all of them. When he arrived at the Pratt household he had no idea when it was appropriate to enter a conversation, he did not know when and how to the use the phone in a way that respected other people, he said the wrong thing at the wrong time, he did not knock on doors when he should, and he was too meek in other situations. He had no sense of boundaries.

Lonni found this extremely disturbing. One night, very late, she heard him on the telephone with a woman he was dating. He wasn't quite screaming, but he wasn't using his inside voice either. He was also using language that Lonni did not appreciate hearing when she woke up in the middle of the night.

She went to him and said, "Your conversation is over now. Hang up the phone and go back to bed. Never do this again or I will have to hurt you." Lonni says he didn't do it again, and she hopes it is because she calmly gave him simple directions to follow, and explained that there would be consequences if he trampled on her boundaries one more time.

While they had this guest at their home, Lonni had a chance to compare his complete failure to understand boundaries with one of the monks who has a full set of well-managed boundaries.

She was researching a writing project and had mentioned it to her friend Brother Damien (now Father Damien). He was in seminary. He suggested that she visit the library on campus, because he thought she would find the specific collection of theological journals that she needed. He offered to take her to campus with him so she could do her research in the morning, and then they would have lunch nearby.

On campus were a couple of things he was sure she would enjoy seeing—the chapel, for example, and the grounds that are lovely to walk. While she was in the library she noticed he would stick his head in the door every now and then, between classes, just to check on her. He never approached her, never interrupted what she was doing. He was comfortable enough to give her space to finish her work. He left it to her to decide when she wanted to see the chapel and when they would take a walk. He could not have been more respectful of boundaries.

Lonni said, "It was a fascinating contrast to our guest who did not have a clue how to honor the boundaries of others or function within personal boundaries. The contrast became even clearer over lunch."

Damien ordered an egg dish with vegetables. When it arrived there was ham in it.

It was Lent, and he had given up meat for Lent. He looked at the steaming dish in front of him and said, "If this passes my lips—it's over," and he made a slicing motion at his neck. He called back the waitress and insisted that she take it back and bring him what he had ordered. He wanted a new entrée; they were not merely to remove the ham from this one.

Father Damien has worked in food service running a family restaurant. He took the word "service" very seriously. Incompetence in service, a lack of consideration for the people you serve, the failure to respect the clear wishes and needs of others—all of these were simply unacceptable. Damien has well-established boundaries. He will not allow others to trample all over him, yet he is one of the most open and giving people you could ever meet.

Being a person with strong and wise boundaries does not make you selfish. It is refusing to let others have boundaries that makes you selfish; it is insisting that others must make *you* the center of their lives that is selfish.

Maintaining boundaries is how we remain hospitable and accepting of ourselves. We said earlier that none of us will ever have a better relationship with another human being than the one we have with ourself. One way to nurture a healthy sense of the self is to keep strong boundaries. People who like themselves tend to maintain boundaries quite naturally.

While it is important that we remain open and available, none of us is a public place either. Denying what we really and truly need, in some misunderstood notion about being hospitable toward others, or loving with others, is simply bad for you. You need time to yourself. You need respect.

Boundaries allow us to give more to others, not less. Boundaries do not exclude the other; in fact, if you become a person with actual boundaries, you are better able to give to other people because you do not feel diminished by it. Giving is a joy because you want to give, and not because someone has manipulated you and you gave in.

Boundaries keep us from feeling used or manipulated. When we set perimeters and refuse to allow ourselves or others to be violated, we become free to enjoy giving. We become free to experience a certain glee in giving joy to others.

A few years ago, after the publication of their first book, Father Dan and Lonni's editor was visiting the monastery with his wife. That editor happened to work for an old, very respected Catholic press. Father Thomas, a monk visiting from Sri Lanka, absolutely loved that Catholic press. He considered anything they published to be next in authority only to Rome. As much as Dan liked the editor, he didn't agree with Father Thomas. But he saw an opportunity to give a great deal of joy to his brother monk.

Lonni remembers that after mass she wanted to introduce Father Dan to the editor's wife, but when she looked for him, he was gone. Most of the monks spent time with their visitors making conversation, drinking coffee, and eating doughnuts. Dan was usually included in that number. Father Thomas, being quite shy, usually went to his room and did not mix with the guests. If you caught him alone, he was delighted to talk to you, but he didn't do crowds very well.

While she was waiting for Dan, suddenly there was Father Thomas heading straight toward their guests, beaming like a silly kid who got what he wanted for Christmas. Lonni described him as "animated," something she had never seen before. He just kept shaking the hand of the tall, quiet editor, who was by then wearing a wide grin. You can't imagine how out of character this was for the monk from Sri Lanka. He shook the editor's hand, he talked, he commended him with booming enthusiasm. Meeting someone from such a highly esteemed Catholic press was sheer delight for Father Thomas, something he could have never expected.

Moments later, Lonni saw Dan. He had obviously gone to Father Thomas and told him the identity of the guest. Then he changed from his habit and joined the fun, enjoying with a twinkle in his eye every moment that Father Thomas beamed at the editor while vigorously and endlessly shaking the man's hand. He had set up Father Thomas for joy.

Hospitality will give the other a handful of joy, if it's possible to do, and that kind of hospitality gives you more bliss than you've given someone else. It is a good reminder that hospitality does not violate you; it doesn't mean you have to be a martyr. Instead it can make you very happy. But you can't give yourself to others when there is no clear sense of a self.

The monk is under constant pressure today to make himself more available to those outside of the monastery. Just as you are not a public place, neither is a monastery. Wouldn't you think that would be clear?

It isn't. Dan can tell dozens of stories about intruders who walk in as if the monastery were a public library, right into the monk's living space. These aren't friends of the monks; they are more like tourists who want a picture of a monk. Father Dan tells a little about one recurring problem with intruders.

The monastery has had a long-standing, recurring problem with teenagers coming to the monastery in the middle of the night to rip up the grass by spinning their car tires and to chase each other through the woods. Sometimes these teenagers have gone into the retreat house or the monastery.

They come from a nearby small city where students have passed around a story about the monks from one class to the next. The rumor they tell is that the monks are dangerous devilish men who perform evil rites, hold people captive, and chase innocent teenagers through the woods with knives and axes. Makes you think they've watched too many bad movies.

The monks and retreatants have been the targets of vandalism, gunshots, and much unacceptable, old-fashioned rudeness. Dan says they have tried everything to combat these problems. They invite the students into the retreat so they can see what is going on, hoping they will understand. They don't; they only cause trouble.

"We've tried reasoning with them, we've tried threatening them with the local police, we've called their parents. The sheer nerve of these kids infuriates me. They think nothing of entering our property for the purposes of destruction, violation, and stirring up trouble," Dan says.

The monks have become adept at rounding up the kids and hauling them inside the retreat house for lecturing and scolding until the police arrive. Father Dan has given interviews to the high school newspaper in that little city, explaining who the Benedictine monks are and what they are doing with all those teenagers in the retreat house. He has hoped that information would end the stupidity.

Finally, the monks put up high gates and locked them. They found no other solution to the problem. This is what every person with a healthy sense of self does at times. We lock out the threat. We refuse to let the destructive thing come close.

The monks cannot hold to their way of life if they overlook the monastic requirement for some cloistered space, some separation and silence. To be fully present to the guest, they must continue, first of all, to be monks. They cannot lose their distinction as Benedictines. This has become increasingly challenging for them as the public has appeared at their chapel, in their walkways, and wandering the paths around the monastery.

You, too, will wrestle with issues of privacy and personal space. You have commitments to keep, and these commitments shape your life. You dishonor yourself, and the people who love you, if you fail to keep your commitments while chasing after a spiritual ideal such as hospitality.

Becoming a hospitable person and keeping your life in balance is not without its complications. Monasticism is a gift to the world only as it keeps its distinction. You're also distinctive. You must remain who you are, and allow yourself to grow more yourself every day. Hospitality will help that happen, it is one of many things that will help that happen, but you must remain freely yourself. If you lose your distinctiveness, the world has lost something it will never see again—you.

Words like *accepting* and *allowing* are a bit misleading. They suggest passivity, as if you are going to become more yourself by doing nothing, and that isn't so. You walk the line between insisting on your right to be yourself, and doing nothing, to become more real.

It's the same struggle the monks face. They must not lose who they are—that would be a monstrous loss to the entire world—but neither can they live in isolation.

The part of us that we give to others, to the stranger you might say, is our outer self. Saying it is an outer self does not mean it is false. It means we reserve our most sacred inner places for those who are trusted to walk gently with us on that soil. With the outer self we give attention. We listen. We offer genuine concern and attempt to enter the experience of someone else. We appreciate the person, and give them something of ourselves, without expecting them to become a friend. We don't necessarily share secrets, inner feelings, dreams, or ambitions and passions.

What we do in hospitality is very important. It does not lessen its importance to admit that it does not go soul deep, because neither is it shallow. The simple courtesy of looking strangers in the eye affirms people. When strangers talk to you they are saying, "Hey, I'm here, I matter, pay attention to me." You build up their humanity when you pay attention.

What does go soul deep is how these seemingly casual encounters of graciousness with others affect you and affect them. They fill the very deep need of the human heart to be heard.

While visiting the monastery Lonni has sometimes had a grandchild or two with her. In one instance she and Father Dan were working on a book project and not paying much attention to the two-year-old. The child was climbing up and down the steps in the retreat house and checking out the bedrooms, as they worked one morning. Suddenly the child had their attention as she yelled, "Look at me, look at me, look at me. . . ." while bolting up and down like a spring, her arms flapping and ponytail swinging. Inside, most of us are still the two-year-old calling out, "Look at me."

It can be emotionally draining to give yourself to someone who has the neediness of a child. These are the people who are most likely to push against your boundaries, and they rarely have boundaries of their own. They are also the most in need of a simple gesture of acceptance. Father Dan recalls meeting just such a person:

"A couple years ago, after the publication of *Benedict's Way: An Ancient Monk's Insights for a Balanced Life,* a reporter from a local radio station wanted to interview us. She came for a preliminary interview. We had given a number of interviews by then and I expected this one would not be much different, until Lonni told me she had something of a history with the reporter. She and the woman had been news editors at competing stations years earlier. It had grown ugly a couple times. Lonni said the woman detested her, but it had been a long time ago. She hoped the other woman had put it in the past."

They were only a few minutes into the interview when it became clear that there was something very wrong with the reporter. She asked *them* what questions she should ask. She was shaking and fumbling. She did not even attempt eye contact. Every now and then her gaze jerked toward Father Dan's face, but she did not look at Lonni.

She giggled at the wrong time, when talking about a tragedy, and then said, "I do know that's not funny.

It's a nervous giggle." When she took their picture for the Web site, she asked them to look at her. She then said to Dan (presumably because he's male), "I know I'm hard to look at but you'll have to try," and then giggled again. She was falling apart in front of them with each passing moment.

The reporter finally brought up her past with Lonni, admitting that they had not liked each other. Lonni agreed that was true, but they had been much younger, she reminded her, and were different people now. The woman looked startled when Lonni said this, as if it were a new concept to her. Lonni's words didn't reassure her. She continued to fall apart as if something about the situation was rocking her to the core.

She seemed to be a bundle of insecurities that would make most people run for the door. Even though she was not someone Dan would have wanted as a friend, he experienced a strong desire to help, to listen to her. He wanted her to understand that she matters. Lonni remembers watching the softening of his eyes as he listened to her, the change in his body language as he tried to reassure her. The kind of caring he wanted to extend to her is typical in hospitality. It is kindness.

People do not need much from us. Actually, they require very little—simple caring really, yet that seems to be more than we have to give. Yes, to be available to those who are needy can cost us emotionally, but we do not offer them our deepest self. If we protect ourselves with appropriate boundaries, we are not threatened by this needy kind of person because they so happily receive whatever little we can give.

We give to meet a need, but giving also soothes our own wounds. You like yourself better after you've reached out to someone like that reporter. Kindness and acceptance are basic to human nature; we need them like we need water and air. We will become less if we don't give it, if we don't receive it. You and I can give a great big bunch of kindness without even coming close to violating boundaries.

Opening up to others does not mean you let someone trample all over you. It does not mean you let people rip chunks off of you. It does not mean you cease to take care of yourself or do what you need to do to remain emotionally, physically, and spiritually healthy. We can give simple kindness without losing ourselves.

nine

Being a Companion Through the Hurt

*L*ife can be deeply painful. No surprise, right? One of the most important ways of extending hospitality is to quietly companion the person who is going through some awful thing. It is no easy thing to be available to the one who is suffering a pain you can't relieve.

Lonni was twenty years old when she watched her first, and at the time only, child die of cancer. Angie's battle had been a short one. At four and a half months the cancer was discovered—she had a tumor on her shoulder—and a mere six months later she was days away from death. In her last days people found it excruciating to be near her. Lonni understood. If there had been a way for her to escape the child's suffering, she says she would have taken it.

Many people wanted to help, however—at least they believed they did. Lonni did not doubt their sincerity. Who could resist the tiny, dark-haired baby with huge blue eyes and a startling ethereal kind of beauty? She was born on Christmas Eve and there had been something special about the child from the first day. Lots of people commented on it. Being in a room with her made you feel better.

Because many people were offering to help, a friend of the family organized a schedule, intending that the baby and Lonni not be left alone in those final frightful days. People signed up for shifts that were supposed to last from two hours to overnight. It was the rare person who lasted a whole night.

Angela was in terrible pain, pain like someone had dropped an anvil on her arm. She was prescribed pain medication to take every four hours to ease the suffering, and the medication did help—a little. About two hours after the dose she would grow restless and begin whimpering. Walking with her, holding her, singing to her, worked to quiet her and comfort her at this point. At about two and a half hours she could not be comforted and did not want to be held. She would lie in her crib and throw her head back and forth, her mouth open, often with no sound coming out as if the pain could not be expressed.

At three hours, she started screaming and trying to rock from side to side in the crib while still lying on her back. No caretaker ever made it past three hours before administering more medication. The baby would calm down, often sleep. But you always knew the crying was coming again.

If the crying didn't get you, the tumor did. She was not a large baby. The tumor on her little shoulder was the size of a large man's fist where it had broken through her china-doll skin. Though bandaged, it wept blood and water constantly. Her arm was engorged to the point of being useless, so when you held her, you had to prop up her arm on your shoulder or support it for her.

People avoided her. We don't deal with the hard realities, such as beautiful children suffering, unless we are forced to. We get through life with some peace of mind by not looking at the hungry children, the dying children, the bombed children, the kids with black eyes and cigarette burns on their legs. It takes a whole lot of courage to do otherwise. In the last few days of her daughter's life a courageous stranger came to stay with them.

"I didn't really know Linda very well," Lonni says. "She was the pastor's wife at a little conservative church one of my friends attended. They were the kind that was rather noisy about their 'born again' religion. I wasn't sure it would work. I imagined her leaving religious materials in my bathroom and scolding me for not praying enough."

But that wasn't Linda. People are always better than the stereotype we try to stuff them into. She had a son who was only weeks older than Angela. Linda showed up one day and she stayed. She made tea and she cooked beef stew. She washed the sheets on all the beds and she handed Lonni a sleeping pill.

As you can imagine, baby clothes didn't fit Angela very well with the huge tumor and engorged arm. The seam of the right sleeve had to be cut open to make her clothing fit. There were a lot of cute little outfits with ripped seams, cute little outfits given as gifts by people like Lonni's mother and grandmother who had dreams for the life of this precious grandbaby.

"Linda was with me when I had to rip the strong seam of a new garment given to us by my grandmother.

being a companion through the hurt | 193

The ripping of the seam matched the ripping in my heart, and as it opened up, so did the deep well of anger and hurt and confusion inside of me. Linda held me as it ruptured the dam and flooded us both.

"In my mind, she is forever framed by the screen door at the back of my little house. I can still see her standing there, trying to make sense of it all, trying to understand what this child's awful suffering said about the world and the God she loved. She had been with us for forty-eight hours. She would remain with me, even after Angela died, until my spouse, who was in the Armed Forces, and family could get there to be with me. Then she would disappear back to her life and I would never see her again.

"That night she looked out into the unseasonably warm October night and said in a shaky voice, 'I don't understand why God allows children to suffer like this. I don't know why this is happening and what it means. But I know this: You can trust a God who bleeds. When you can't trust anything else, you can trust a God who bleeds.' She said the words out loud, but I had the definite impression Linda was talking to herself, rather than me."

Linda's primary Christian image was of a God who gave himself and held nothing back from his Creation, a God who died with the cost of loving. Her availability to Angela and Lonni grew naturally out of her deep faith.

Linda stood beside Lonni during the darkest time of her life. She opened her heart knowing for sure it was going to get broken. Being with them would force her to look right into the face of realities and doubts she had been able to avoid, until she held the dying baby and thought of her own son. In becoming available to them, she paid a high price emotionally and spiritually.

"I don't know how I would have survived without Linda," Lonni says. "She became the face of God to me when God seemed gone. I could not find a way to pray, or believe in a good God. I could not get past the anger and doubt, but I could hold onto this woman. I wasn't sure how to take the next breath, but I could take her love and feel her love. I didn't have to give back anything. Good thing, because I wasn't capable of it. I could let her take care of us. It was the hardest time I've ever known and during it, God's name was Linda."

That's what we can be for one another when we open our hearts—the very presence of God. During the national memorial service to honor those lost in the September 11 attacks, some people spoke of one woman who prayed a televised prayer, "God give us a sign that you're still here."

The sign that God is still here is the goodness we rediscovered in one another. God was still here when people escorted Muslim mothers and children on their daily errands. These were some of the signs that God is still with us.

"We are here to be God's presence to you," is what a bishop said to a grieving family at a funeral recently. When people are bent over with the weight of suffering, they need from us only our presence. If we give them that, truly give them that, we become for them the presence of God in a most tangible way. That is hospitality.

The situation does not have to be as dramatic as what happened with Linda. Few of us will ever be involved in such a life-shattering situation. But we can be present in everyday ways to those who hurt and those who are shunned. We can make a pot of chili and take it to a single mother or offer to baby-sit for a single father. We can mow the grass of the man who is recovering from heart surgery, or play checkers with the old woman who has cancer and will not last another month.

There is no shortage of pain you can relieve. But you know, just as Linda knew, that it is going to be costly. You will barely escape with your own self. And, whatever sense of self and the world you get out with, it will never be the same. You can't engage with human pain and remain unchanged. But that is the beauty of it. It will cost you everything and you will gain everything.

When we say we become God's presence and that something beautiful emerges from the suffering, we aren't saying that God makes these things happen so that we will reap these results, like benefits in some nightmarish cosmic insurance policy. Events happen because freedom allows events to happen; they happen on their own, and the randomness of it all can be heart-stopping. God is present in the awful thing—not as its origin, but as the One who even in the most skin-crawling and torturous of events, offers the miraculous possibility of healing and a new beginning.

In his book *Voices of Silence*, Frank Bianco tells the story of Bede, a rather stuck-in-a-rut Trappist monk. It was in the post–Vatican II days, when monasteries all over the country were struggling to find ways to be more open to laity. This particular monk was against such a thing.

"There will be women in shorts running around," he grumbled. He had gone to the monastery to avoid women in shorts. But he couldn't stop the strong hand of the Spirit throwing open locked doors in those days, and the laity and the women showed up.

One day Bede was praying in the chapel. From behind him, in the area roped off for visitors, he heard a young woman crying. Her cry pierced his brittle heart, and before he knew what he was doing, he was heading toward the area roped off for visitors.

When he reached the velvet cord, he grabbed it almost in anger. He knew now that love was never meant to be bound. Unhooking the rope, he half-flung it to the floor and moved toward the pew.

The young woman who sat there had not heard him approaching.

"Please," he asked, "is there anything I can do?'"

She looked up into his face, seeing what she would later describe as an exact copy of her father's face, only older. Her father had cancer and she feared for his life. The father she adored might soon be gone. She did not know how she would live the rest of her life without him. She hated how the cancer was hurting him.

The monk soon discovered that the young woman was his granddaughter, which neither the monk nor the girl had known. He had been in a relationship and had intended to marry a young woman before World War II, but had gone off to war. While he was gone her family had forbidden her to marry him. She was expecting a child by then—his son. He went straight from the war to the monastery without ever looking back.

Bede did not know his son was looking for him and believed he was in a monastery in Massachusetts (Bede was actually in Kentucky). Then, the son received a call from his daughter saying she had met a monk "who could easily be your twin if you were twenty years older."

If the monk had kept his heart clenched, he would never have known his granddaughter and would not have been able to be with his son, nursing him back to health. Bede died in a car accident shortly after returning to the monastery following his leave of absence.

He had to overcome all his worst fears to get past the ropes that kept the suffering girl at a distance. Once he got past the barriers there was no turning back; everything was different. Do you think he ever regretted it?

In taking on the pain of others we act in the transformation of the world. We ourselves are changed, and we make a small push against the darkness. We make a difference. Benedict wanted his monks to make a difference.

We can be hospitable to others in very ordinary ways. When we are companions through the hurt, chances are it will cost us emotionally. If we care for the dying, eventually we'll lose our hearts to someone who is dying. If we work in a shelter for battered women and their children, one of these days someone is going to get through the thickest of skin. We can't feed the hungry without asking the hard questions about why there is hunger. This kind of hospitality will extract everything from us, leaving us stripped of our pretty delusions.

Through the years a lot of young people have taken their broken dreams and disheveled young lives to Subiaco retreat house at St. Benedict Monastery for repair. Not long ago the monks found a young woman in their chapel who had been on retreat at the monastery in her teens. It turned out that she had gone into the dark, empty retreat house the night before and slept in one of the bedrooms. Like many young adults she had gone home for the holidays. But the difference with her was that her mother didn't want her home. The girl just wanted to be near the place she still considered home, so she returned anyway and ended up at the monastery.

The young woman's family story is one of the worst you can imagine. During some of the worst times of her teen years she had sat on one of the big rocks lining the monastery driveway. She felt safe there, welcome, and loved. She felt like the world made some sense.

Through tears she told the monks, "I just had to come back and sit on my rock and sleep in the retreat house again." Father Dan says this happens more than he ever imagined it would.

It is not unusual that when life becomes strained and confusing, the former teen-retreatants, now in their twenties and thirties, head back to a place where they felt sheltered. Some of the former teens stay in touch and become friends of the monastery. Others just reappear one day in profound emotional distress. A while back, one young man showed up in such a state. He wanted to see both Father Dan and Mary Cummings. There was no way that was possible without him joining the teen retreat, even though the man was closing in on thirty years old.

"Neither of us minded," Dan said. "We knew from experience that his presence was going to complicate things, though. He would need attention from us and it would be emotionally exhausting. We needed to be at our strongest for the teens on retreat. It wasn't the first time such a thing had happened. We thought we knew what to expect."

He said they could not have prepared themselves for how far into despair the man had tumbled. His emotional state required that one of them be with him, almost constantly. Both Dan and Mary were afraid he would hurt himself if left alone. Throughout the weekend, they took shifts being with the teens, and being with the man curled up with his pain in a back bedroom.

During the visit, this friend attended the Office of Prayer with the monks. One night at Vespers he began sobbing. His whole body shook, and it was clear that something had broken and was now available for healing.

"We were at Vespers, our evening prayer, and we were standing while chanting. The whole time he was sobbing, we kept chanting and praying. You could almost see the prayer wrapping around him, surrounding him with strength and righting something inside of him that needed righting. While it was very tempting, every monk there knew it was the wrong time to take him aside and question him or attempt to comfort him. Instead, we did what we monks do. We kept our hand to the task and we prayed. In what is ordinary to us, his healing began."

It is the ordinary things we do to care for others that will make a difference in the most difficult of situations. Suffering is inconvenient. It alters our plans. It takes a swipe at us when we are not looking. None of us likes or welcomes the sudden interruption or change that alters everything.

But hospitality is not a planned event, or a series of routine gestures. It is the stance of the heart that is abandoned to Love. In monasticism, this ability to remain open to the Other is fed by the monastic vow of stability.

For practical purposes the vow of stability has to do with staying physically in one place. A Benedictine monk can expect to live his life and die in one place—the monastery. There is a singleness of purpose to a life of stability; some questions are resolved once and for all. Stability is harder to come by if you have not taken a vow.

Change is the constant that most people live with and expect. Because any interruption in the course of events is just another change in a long line of interruptions and changes, we sometimes find it difficult to welcome the interruption. We so much want to lay plans and have them work. The seeming randomness of the universe leaves us feeling helpless, so we grasp at control.

One way to come to terms with these kinds of interruptions is to clean up as many loose ends in your life as you can. You will feel more relaxed and able to be with someone when you are not scooting through the day in fifteen-minute increments. Don't overplan your day. Cut your schedule to as few activities as possible. Keep it simple, and plan to be interrupted.

Every person we know has more than enough of everything. Another way to free up time and give the soul a chance to relax is to unload some of the stuff you've collected. If all you do is dust it, maybe it should find another home. There is nothing wrong with owning and enjoying. But sometimes we forget that enough is enough.

If we have not worn it for a couple years, give it to someone who will wear it. If we have not read it, viewed it, listened to it anytime recently, why store it and dust it?

What we accumulate gets inside of us. Life is enough to manage without having to manage so much irrelevant stuff too. Simplify. Now be careful about this. You can also complicate simplification. Dozens of books exist on the subject, and you can even attend conferences on how to simplify. Fine, if it helps. Most people can simplify life by just being honest with themselves and deciding what matters most.

In addition to simplifying as much as possible, making promises and keeping promises will free us to be more open to others. Commitment brings with it a great deal of freedom because, by its nature, it closes down options. We have become a people of too many options. Really now, how many brands of shampoo does one nation need?

Commitment can do for us what stability does for the monk. Commitment means we are going to show up tomorrow for work and will keep the same spouse we live with today. The more committed we are to our family, friends, and our convictions, the more free we become to be open to others. Commitment settles us down and makes room inside for another to enter. It resolves crucial decisions such as whom I will love and where I will live and what I will do with my life. By closing up some options, commitment frees you to live in peace with yourself. It quiets the struggles.

Over time, as our life becomes more stable, we can begin to see the stranger less as a disruption and more as a gift. The stranger is a lot like God, after all. God is constantly disrupting our best plans, God shows up when it is less than convenient, God is present no matter what we do to shoo him off. How we live with all these strangers who keep messing up our plans will determine the future for all of us.

We don't have to have all the answers to companion the hurting. Actually people who try to offer answers are not particularly comforting. Do we really think it would hurt less if we understood? Forget answers. Be available. Be available with eyes wide open. Know it is going to interrupt your well-planned life.

This kind of hospitality moves you past yourself, helps you to transcend yourself. To put aside my own pain and feel yours is truly a magical power. It is a power that can eventually transform the world into a place where no one is excluded and no tear goes uncomforted.

ten

Listening: The Deep Truth of Hospitality

"Listen to me!" This is the primal call of the human heart. In the movie *What Women Want*, Mel Gibson plays a character who suddenly acquires the ability to hear women thinking. When interviewed, the woman who wrote the movie said, "What women want is what all people want— they want someone to listen."

There is nothing that more characterizes the Benedictine life than listening. It has been called the key to Benedict's entire spiritual teaching. More than anything else, a monk is called to be a listener. All of his days, the monk is trained to hear God. He learns to hear God in everything and everyone.

To Benedict, listening is not the same as intellectual comprehension. Listening, as Benedict understood it, is a special kind of deep attentiveness to all of life. Benedict understood that we can live in ways that either dull or sharpen this attentiveness. Benedict's *Rule* is a guide to sharpening the ears of the heart.

The place of listening in monasticism cannot be overemphasized. The monk who is not listening is missing the point. Kathleen Norris, author of *Cloister Walk*, tells a story about talking to one of her monk friends. They were in his office and she was trying to express something that mattered very much to her. But as she talked, she noticed he was preoccupied. After a few minutes of watching him be distracted and restless, she snapped at him, "Will you listen to me please!" Listen. Ah. She had the Benedictine's attention. Listen, yes, that's what it is I'm supposed to be doing.

Many years ago Lonni and her family lived across the street from a little log cabin. The place was abandoned and in rather rough shape. One autumn, a man moved into the cabin. Lonni's husband, David, being the outgoing type he is, went over and introduced himself. Lonni, being the introvert she is, did not. Upon his return from the first visit with their new neighbor, Les,

David reported that Les was going to fix up the place and sell it.

Lonni didn't think much more about Les until a few nights later when screaming suddenly cut through the peace of the neighborhood. Horrible screaming, the kind that drives you into a fetal position if you hear it for too long. Lonni got out of bed and went to a bedroom window that was opened just a bit. The screams were coming from the little log house. They were not actually all that loud—loud enough to hear, but not ear-piercing. It was the suffering that was so loud. They were the screams of a grown man.

The next night, Lonni woke up to his screams again. And the next. Then silence for several nights before the screams happened again.

One day, Lonni came home from the office for lunch. It was a cool October day. She took a bowl of chili and a thermos of coffee and some apple cake to Les. She introduced herself. He was a soft-spoken man who looked a bit like Willie Nelson with less hair. Lonni didn't ask him about the screaming and he didn't bring up the subject either.

He talked about a marriage that failed and said he would never marry again. He told her that he had fixed up quite a few old houses. He lived in them, repaired them, sold them to "nice young families for a good price," and then he moved on. And finally, as he drained the last of the coffee he talked of Vietnam. He said, "I'll never get out of those fields."

Les never said the words, but he asked Lonni to understand his screaming. He asked her to give him a chance to repair the house and move a nice family into it. He asked her to be the kind of neighbor who will smile at you in the morning after you have spent the night screaming against the dark. He took a chance by telling her his story and asking her to accept him and live for a season with his suffering. But he never said any of that.

Winter shut the windows and the drapes in the quiet neighborhood. Lonni didn't hear his screams as often, but when insomnia hit, she would sometimes hear something coming from the locked windows across the street and she would pray for the man who could never stay in one place, because he could never forget another place.

Everything changes when you hear the screams in the night. You can't be the same after that—and if that doesn't make you cross the street with a bowl of chili and a heart ready to listen, nothing will.

When we learn to listen, we will hear screams, and the sound of another's suffering changes everything. It unsettles us, breaks apart our comfort, and makes us choose a side. We become less human when we decide to do nothing once we have heard the screams. Years of ignoring the pain around us makes us less able to respond. This is one way we become hard and closed. It isn't easy to stay open. God knows it isn't easy.

You can go along day after day, hour after hour, without hearing much of anything and then something slams into you and gets your attention. Some equivalent of a scream in the night. You didn't expect it, sure didn't want it, but it strikes you with such power when your guard is down that you end up listening, despite not wanting to hear another's pain.

One day when Father Dan was visiting his mother in a nursing home, one of the physical therapists taking care of his mother commented that she seemed rather depressed that day. His mother sighed and said, "Who the hell wouldn't be depressed?" She was right. You can't live sanely in this world without a heart that is breaking for yourself, and all of us, in this whole big mess. We are all lost together. We choose our own destruction rather than life. We know this is the truth and who the hell wouldn't be depressed about it?

You know it's true because every now and then you've listened enough to hear the truth. You have seen more than you've let on. Through moments of blinding beauty and deafening pain you have heard the *more* that runs through it all.

Benedict calls us to hear the *more*. Listen, the ancient monk tells us, listen. It will break you heart, but it will also give you a heart. And it will give you more—it will give you life. Only Love is strong enough to hold all the pain in the world. Love will listen. If you aren't listening, you aren't loving.

Listening is always involved in hospitality. The most gracious attempts we can muster are meaningless if we do not actually hear the stranger. Listening is the core meaning of hospitality. It is something we can give anyone and everyone, including ourselves. It takes only a few minutes to really listen.

A young man who worked all during his high school years bagging groceries said that the vast majority of people who went through his line never looked at him when he asked, "Paper or plastic?" He said people did not meet his eyes, smile at him, or acknowledge him in any way. What a tiny thing. Look up; look into the eyes of the young person and smile.

The former bag-boy said, "My mother asked me one day why I always hung around her, talking, after work. I didn't know why until Mom and I talked about how I feel at work. I feel like I'm not quite human."

This is what happens to the one who feels as if no one ever listens. Most of us cannot imagine such an existence, but there are homes and places where people are not heard. Children are often not listened to; they are viewed as objects to be maintained rather than real human beings.

A young couple was in a restaurant with their four-year-old son. They were being waited on by one of those experienced waitresses who never show contempt for a customer, but by their unhurried pace and level gaze make it evident they fear no mortal, not even parents. She jotted on her pad, deliberately and quietly, while the parents gave their selections, including substitutions and such. She turned to the boy and he began his order in a kind of fearful desperation.

"I want a hot dog," he started. His parents barked in unison, "No hot dog!" The mother scowled at the boy, who fell silent, and said, "Bring him the vegetable and grilled chicken, milk and. . . "

The waitress ignored the parents as she looked directly at the boy. "What do you want on your hot dog?"

The amazed child said, "Lots of ketchup, and a pickle, too. And could you bring some milk?"

"Coming up," she said and turned from the table, never even looking at the stunned parents. The boy watched her depart with astonished delight and then said to his dismayed parents, "You know what? She thinks I'm real! She thinks I'm real!"

That's how you feel when someone listens to you: Real.

Every person is born with the right to become exactly who they were created to be. When a human being isn't heard, when all that is special to a child is ignored so that the child can be shaped into what the parents think the child should be—that person is in grave danger of becoming less than they were made for.

Hospitality is a way to counter the thousands of times another human being has felt less than human because others didn't listen. Listening is the power of hospitality; it is what makes hospitality the lifegiving thing it is. When you listen, you get past yourself too. That is something we all need to do a little more. In the listening stance, the focus switches from the self to the other.

Every now and then we meet someone who is very good at listening. When people have been with someone who really listens, they feel better about themselves. "I feel like someone is listening to me for the first time," a number of people have said about their association with the monks of St. Benedict Monastery. There is nothing more human than our desire to be heard. It is our cry for permission to live.

The woman in the grocery store who talks about how her toddler isn't potty-trained yet. The old man who talks about how often it has snowed in March since 1921. The man who tells the same old joke every time you see him. The woman who never ceases discussing her health problems. What all of these people have in common is that they are looking for someone to affirm them and give them permission to be.

There is so much in life that is potentially dehumanizing. Listening is the most hospitable thing we can do, and if we do no other thing than train ourselves to listen to others, we will have taken great steps in hospitality.

One of the local discount stores in our area makes a practice of hiring many disabled persons. Some of them are physically disabled, others are mentally disabled. These special employees tend to be given the task of putting your new sweatshirt, socks, and cabbage into bags. Watch the people in those lines. Some of them are actually pretty comfortable with the interesting and different people at the end of the line waiting to bag your underwear. Others do everything they can to ignore these people.

Imagine you are in line behind a very nice woman who is clearly uneasy with the young man bagging her purchases. It happened to a friend the other day.

The guy bagging was probably thirty-five, but mentally closer to twelve or thirteen. He was blonde and short with a wide smile. He had a scar across the left temple that was at least three inches long. He probably had not been born with his disability. He wore a name badge that read, "Kevin."

Kevin greeted the woman and said, "Are you in a hurry today?"

She did not look at Kevin. She looked at the woman ringing up her order and managed a faint smile. She said, "The lines are rather long this morning." The woman nodded and kept dashing things through the scanner.

Kevin tried again, "You have a lot of pop here. Are you going to have company?"

The older woman turned toward the person behind her in line, as if looking for help; she had a frantic look in her eye. She was not a mean-spirited woman; she simply had come of age in an era when such a young man would have been institutionalized, rather than commenting on her purchases.

Our friend standing behind her smiled and said, "You do have a lot of pop."

"My grandson is turning fourteen. It's for his party."

"My sister had a birthday party," the disabled young man said. He drooled and it landed on a liter-size bottle of green pop and rolled off. The woman at the register glanced from the drool to the boy and kept working.

"I'll bet that was a lot of fun," said our friend.

Then the woman buying pop for her grandson's party did a courageous thing. It was so brave you wanted to cry for her. She turned toward Kevin, took a breath, and looked him in the eye. She said, "Did you enjoy the party?"

Kevin nodded. "I like parties. My sister says she gets two birthdays a year because I'm such a pain in the butt, so she gets mine." He grinned. "But she don't mean it because she always takes me to the show for my birthday and I get the biggest bag of popcorn." He looked up from his bagging and said, "I love my sister."

The woman blinked back tears. Kevin was only twelve inches from her and he was a real live human being now, and she didn't even want to escape him any longer. She touched his hand and said, "I am certain that she loves you, too."

"Yup, that's why I get the biggest bag of popcorn," he said.

Right there in the checkout line, day after day, are encounters between people like the old woman and Kevin. Sure, you know there is some politically correct employment policy behind the employment of the special people stuffing bags at this discount store, but so what? The result is magic. Humans understanding other humans a little better. Hospitality happens even at Meijers.

Kevin probably gets ignored often, but you know Kevin is used to it. Now that he's out there at the cash register, every now and then someone will look Kevin in the eye and they will affirm him, they will grin at him, they will listen to Kevin. And that would not happen without that politically correct employment policy.

It is very good for Kevin, but if you have known a few people like him you know that he will be okay anyway. There is an ability to love, understand, forgive, and accept in the Kevins of our world that is beyond understanding.

The one who otherwise would have avoided Kevin is the one who is really changed when he first listens, when he first discovers he can no longer ignore someone whose only crime is making him uneasy. Listening is the core of hospitality, and while the people we listen to benefit, in the end we are the ones transformed.

Benedict doesn't call us to listen on the surface. He wants us to listen with the ears of the soul. Listen way down deep. You know the place; it's the same place that weeps at the sight of a newborn, the same place that falls silent at the edge of a mountain, the same place that reaches for a falling sparrow. Listen from *that* place.

Listening is a choice to be receptive, to stop speaking and take an open stance. It involves a patient waiting for the real self to be revealed, even if just a little bit of the real self. Listening means we move past what we think we know, and by listening to someone else's story, we learn something we would not have discovered any other way.

Listening is important because it forms bonds between people and reinforces self-worth. People feel better when they have been listened to. Listening helps us understand how others are different from us, and how they are the same. By really hearing someone, we come to realize that we never perfectly understand anyone. That realization helps us drop the unrealistic expectation that anyone will ever completely understand us. Listening validates the one you listen to; it affirms him and reminds him of his basic worth.

A friend tells the story of his son Paul who was, at the age of eleven, taken to meet his great-aunt in a nursing home where she had been moved from out of state. Aunt Margaret was in the advanced stages of dementia. She was, however, thrilled to see Paul. She touched his face and stroked his hair and held his hands while she told him stories that were eighty-five years old, stories of being a girl almost a century ago.

As she talked and talked, the father grew concerned that his son's lesson in respect and kindness was going to be ruined by her endless "when I was a girl" chattering. He interrupted with an excuse and got Paul out of there. On the way to the car he tried to explain dementia to his son. Paul stopped him and said, "Hey, Dad, you don't have to make excuses for Aunt Margaret. She was just remembering who she is."

Listening is at the heart of Benedictine spirituality because it is the only way to see through the eyes of another. When we listen to another, we catch a slight glimpse of their soul. We create an open page where they are free to write their story. We help people remember who they are.

A friend of Lonni's told us a story about the day her husband called to tell her he wanted to bring home a guest, a woman from South Africa. She told him no, don't even think about it, buster. It could not have been a worse day, she explained.

The washing machine had busted and she was out of diapers, so the babies had dishtowels pinned to their bottoms (they were the parents of boys, two sets of twins, aged two and five). There were no clean towels and the beds were stripped and all she had were soggy sheets. She explained that she planned to serve boxed macaroni and cheese and hot dogs on paper plates for dinner. She told him that she had not had time for a shower and did not see any break in her schedule for that particular luxury before midnight.

What's more, when the dishtowels on the babies' bottoms became soiled she would be stripping them down to naked.

"'No,' I told him, 'do not bring this woman home, not today.' He begged. He said we were exactly what she wanted to see, a normal American family. I pointed out that not many American families had a lunatic for a mother, and two sets of twins, and he just laughed. He said she would love hot dogs and the twins and the paper plates and even little lunatic me. I gave in."

That night over paper plates and boxed macaroni the woman, her husband, and their four sons heard the stories of apartheid. The mother knew the youngest two would not remember them, but she determined, before the meal was over, she would tell the stories to her sons again and again. She would not let them forget. The guest had once had her own sons, two of them. They had both been killed in the violence.

The guest helped clean up, she helped put the children to bed, and then she sat on their front porch steps and cried while she smoked one cigarette after another.

"She was a child of God who had lost her way," said Lonni's friend. "She didn't know if she would ever go home again. She told me weeks later, she opened her heart to a white woman for the first time in years. She wasn't the only one who was changed that night, though. I learned the stranger comes to me with the message of an angel, a gift to give me that will change my life."

Hospitality is a way to take the gift of life seriously. We hear a great deal of talk about the sanctity of life, but we see few people living in a way that celebrates it. By our best and worst attempts at hospitality we say to ourselves and to the whole world:

> Everything matters.
> You are not alone.
> You are more than you know.
> The awful thing is not the final word.
> Today is all we have and today is enough.
> We need each other.

On one of Lonni's first visits to help with the teen retreats at the monastery, she met a teenaged girl who had just been through the death of a friend. She was not a participant of the retreat; she just showed up on Saturday morning because she needed to be with friends to grieve.

Father Dan knew the girl; he also had known and loved the girl who died. The retreat house was jammed with teens. In addition, more adults had accompanied the youth than usual. It was crowded and they had a schedule to keep, goals to accomplish, youth to guide and help.

"What amazed me that weekend," Lonni recalls, "was not the way the staff made all the teens feel special, even though they did. What amazed me was how tenderly Dan stood beside one teenager who was having a tough time. And she was not a retreat kid. She was a drop-in. But that was okay. Sometimes you need to be where you'll be understood."

Lonni did not witness many conversations between the two of them. She witnessed Father Dan listening to someone's grief in a profound, but subtle, way. The monk was present to the girl in small ways, sitting with her, hanging up her coat, pouring her Pepsi, touching her hand at just the right moment. It was not some skill he had learned; it is just who he is, who he has become through the years of following the Benedictine path.

Becoming a person of hospitality is not just a matter of learning Benedictine ideas and then applying those ideas. That's a pretty good place to start—but truly learning them takes a lifetime. You will not even know when it happens—that is how natural being hospitable will eventually seem.

During a three-city book tour Lonni had the chance to see that she had a long way to go before becoming as hospitable as Father Dan. They were on the third city of the tour. Both of them were close to collapsing with exhaustion. They had been invited to visit a center for retired Benedictine nuns on Sunday. Dan gave the homily at mass, and they had breakfast with some of the sisters. Lonni was hoping for a nap after that. She says the world would have seemed like a better place after a nap.

"But a nap was not in my near future. Instead, I found myself on a tour with a couple of the staff, also Benedictine nuns, who wanted to introduce us to each and every nun in the whole place. This did not improve my attitude, I promise you. I was pretty locked up inside of myself, not paying much attention to the sisters as we moved from room to room.

"I'm not sure which sister got my attention, but in the course of our introductions one of the nuns reached out and took Dan's hand and took mine. I was jerked back from the selfish depths of myself long enough to notice that Father Dan was connecting—I mean intentionally pushing past his exhaustion to connect with every single person he met. He asked them questions and sincerely listened to them. He laughed with them and he touched them. He was available even in a state of fatigue."

There was some deep well, some resource, he was drawing from, a place she had not yet discovered in herself. It reminded her of the story of Jesus meeting the woman at the well. Tired, hungry, and weary—that is what the Savior of the world was that day. He was in a place nice Jewish boys did not go, talking to the kind of woman Mary probably would have told him to avoid. It is one of the liveliest conversations recorded in the Gospels. They banter, they engage, they chide, and they connect. The Lord of the Universe is enjoying himself because he's got a live one.

Jesus hears her, really hears her, in a way no other person has ever heard her. She tells other people that he has understood her in a way no other person ever understood her. It is such a remarkable thing for her and it costs this dear Jesus so much. His followers return and urge him to eat, to keep up his strength. He tells them that he is fed from a place they do not understand.

"That day," Lonni says, "watching Father Dan, the monk, I wondered if I could ever do what he was doing. I hoped, fiercely hoped, that someday I would be able to. Much later, I told him how impressed I was with what I'd seen him do, and he gave me this weird look and changed the subject. It came so naturally to him that he was not aware of what a remarkable thing he did."

You have probably heard news stories about the brilliant inventor Dean Kamen. Some people think his high-tech motorized scooter will change transportation and even alter the way cities are designed. What few know about Kamen is that he also invents revolutionary medical devices.

He has invented, for example, a wheelchair that can navigate stairs without any special equipment. The same wheelchair also allows the person sitting in it to raise the seat so that he or she can look other people in the eye. Sounds like a pretty amazing piece of equipment, doesn't it?

We can do even more amazing and profound things for one another. Nothing will keep the pain from crippling each one of us from time to time. We cannot escape that reality. But we can help each other climb the difficult stairs of our lives; we can help each other when moving under our own steam just is not going to happen. We can raise each other up in dignity, and look right into one another's eyes. We can help each other make it to places that have been closed to us.

Lonni tells a story about our efforts to hear one another from her days of sitting in a hospital waiting room:

> When my infant daughter was being treated for cancer we spent a lot of time in a waiting room at Children's Hospital in Detroit. The babies and toddlers, the kids and the teens, all waited in that room for a turn at having chemicals put into a vein in the desperate hope of stopping cancer in its

listening: the deep truth of hospitality | 229

tracks. Parents, relatives, and friends waited with the children.

I was there with my little baby; often my father was with me. It's not spoken, but we have something like assigned seats in that place and somehow we all find out one another's story. I don't recall much talking about cancer, but we heard each other in other ways, ways I don't remember anymore.

On this particular day one of the chairs is empty and we all know what that means. It means one of us isn't coming back. One of us is gone. Another one has lost. That makes the waiting room quiet.

I'm not the only young mother in the room. There's one next to me with her son Matthew. Matthew is a year old. He's very thin with sticks for arms and legs. He has the largest eyes you will ever see on a child. He's bald. Most of the kids are bald. Chemo.

Across from Matthew is a teenaged girl, probably fourteen or fifteen. She, too, wears a stocking cap. Matthew's is red, hers is navy blue. The girl has been there since before Angie and I started in the waiting room. She's curled up in her chair in something like a fetal position. In any other place on the planet, people would be very concerned about what she is doing and how she looks. Here—well, here nothing is like anywhere else on the planet. She is with her aunt, because her single father won't go to the hospital with her. It is too hard for him to bear, he says.

Matthew's mother puts him on the floor. Show time. He pulls himself up to standing, using one of the orange plastic chairs to balance, and then he lets go and just stands there wobbling. He has our attention. When a child like Matthew does something as ordinary as take his first steps, it is good news in a place like this, a sign of hope. We cling to every crumb of hope.

The girl is watching. She doesn't want you to notice, but she's untangled those long, skinny arms and legs of hers and is slouched in the chair now, peering at wobbling Matthew from under her stocking cap. Matthew's sky-blue gaze fixes on the girl. He waves his arms and he's off—walking, really walking, while his mother beams at this never-before-seen event.

He takes seven steps to the girl. I count them. He bumps into her bony knees, slaps his hands down on her legs, and looks up at her with a great big grin and grunt of triumph. Magic. Her face is changing, transforming into a smile that reaches her young eyes and makes her pretty again. She speaks. Another first.

"Can I hold him?" she asks the mother.

"Sure."

She scoops up the baby into her arms, "Well, Mr. Matthew, aren't you something!" she says softly and snuggles him tight to her caved-in chest. He relaxes against her, tucks his head under her chin, and spreads his arms wide open around her shoulders. He takes a deep breath and exhales. He goes limp. They sit there like that, the two of them. It's hard to tell who is holding who.

They have found their way home to each other. They have heard each other when no one said a word. Their connection is the same one we all share—our frail humanity. We do so need each other, and doesn't it terrify us?

With all its unforgettable beauty, this is still a sometimes dark and sometimes shuddering world we live in. We recognize this, no more profoundly than when we discuss such things as children living and dying with cancer, or the horrors of terrorism.

It is a courageous thing to keep getting up every day, and it is a much more courageous thing to rouse your heart and incline it to love. To care for each other, to open the door to the stranger, to open your heart to the stranger, lifts you up into the great dance of life.

There is a wider way, a higher way. To go this way we must keep our hearts open to the possibility of serendipity in the eyes of the stranger. God is among us. In a world where we see only in part and know even less, it is hard to spot God. Our eyes are not trained to see any better than our ears are trained to listen. It is not important that we recognize God in the stranger; God is there whether we notice or not. We can just assume that fact and do the next thing—accept the stranger.

What matters is that we stretch our hearts open and draw near to each other. It is the way of hospitality, the way of life, and it is, in this remote place where we have awakened to find ourselves, the only way home.

Discover more about the wisdom of St. Benedict

A Good Life
Benedict's Guide to Everyday Joy
Robert Benson
85 pages
ISBN: 1-55725-356-0
$13.95 Trade Paper

What makes a "good life" in today's fast-paced, competitive world? Beloved author and spiritual guide Robert Benson turns to an unexpected source—the wisdom of St. Benedict, the "father" of Western monasticism.

Compassionate and practical, Benedict created a rule of life—balancing prayer, rest, community, and work—that has helped men and women for centuries to lead more fulfilling lives. With his trademark humor and light-hearted prose, Benson shares his own struggle to balance a spiritual life with the demanding roles of father, husband, and writer. Anyone who feels pulled in too many directions will find in *A Good Life* thoughtful, ancient wisdom for creating a life of deep meaning and joy.

"Like Brother Lawrence and others before him, Robert Benson gently guides readers toward a life of worship, a life in which simple duties take on divine significance. . . . *A Good Life* offers a path toward God-centered living, lit with ancient wisdom and warmed with hope."
—Liz Curtis Higgs, best-selling author of *Bad Girls of the Bible*

Available from most booksellers or through Paraclete Press: www.paracletepress.com; 1-800-451-5006.
Try your local bookstore first.